My Deadly Friend

Steffen Krumm

My Deadly Friend

The chaotic journey of an alcoholic

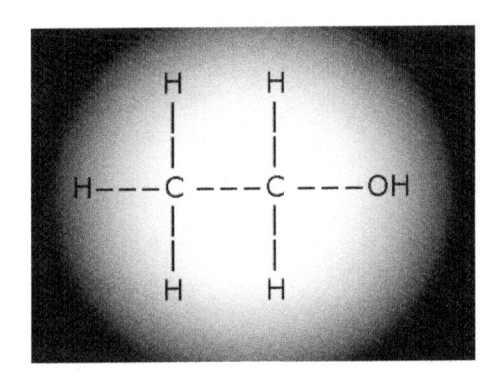

Imprint

Texts: © Copyright by Steffen Krumm Cover: © Copyright by Steffen Krumm

Publisher: **NewDreams Verlag**

Steffen Krumm

Gänsestrasse 22

18311 Ribnitz-Damgarten

Phone: 0176 46604243

Email: *steffenk67@gmail.com*

www.sk-newdreams.de

Table

1. *Preface*
2. *Programming*
3. *The Stranger in Me*
4. *The 90s*
5. *Old "love" new sparks*
6. *Relaxation*
7. *Serrahn*
8. *The Party*
9. *A Star for one day*
10. *Shared suffering*
11. *Hells bells and Angels trompete*
12. *No permanent residence*

13. Station F5

14. Ribnitz-Damgarten

15. My family

16. Thoughts on Addiction

17. "On smooth waves"

18. Thank you very much

Preface

The name of my deadly friend is alcohol! Everyone knows this name, everyone knows what alcohol does, but few know, that you can fall in love with this friend. A long and intense love affair. You build a very strong bond with this friend, from which you just can't let go. He is a comforter in solitude, a savior, an important elixir for body and soul. He calms down, takes inhibitions and ensures a good mood. You can find the right words with him or not. He is fun and can erase pain. He is a place of refuge, he gives you asylum without asking for your origin. A true friend.

But he can do things differently. He persecutes, he destroys, he is murderous and deadly. He deceives you, until you can't get anything on the line without him. My friend even led me to death for a short time! Over the years, he showed his true face. He is cunning, deceptive, powerful and very strong – much stronger than me!

He is so strong that I gave him 25 years of my life. Just like that? No, not just like that. He has the ability to deceive, and he has only one thing in mind, which is to destroy everything that is important, precious and deeply loved by you. Unfortunately, one does not notice his strategy until it is far too late, or -in the worst case- to late at all. In this book, I describe true events that I experienced with this "beautiful"-deadly friend. I have fallen for him again and again – in every situation – and that is exactly what will happen, if I get involved with him again.

What I experienced with him, I tried to describe in a partly funny, moving, frightening, but also in a very sad way.

Some readers may find themselves in some episodes because they have experienced similar things and can understand my stories.

For many readers, my experiences may sound unbelievable or incredible. This is because most people, thank God, are not alcoholic, so it is very difficult for them to understand certain things. This very close relationship with my friend led to countless rescue operations, over a hundred hospital stays including detoxification, six long-term therapies, a helicopter operation and many criminal acts.
He left me with long-term damage that affects both, my psyche and my physical abilities. The aim of this book is to encourage alcoholics to find a way out of this terrible swamp before it is too late. It may also be a therapeutic enrichment for one or the other. But I would also like to try by writing this book – and I think it is really important - to evoke a little understanding among people, who have nothing to do with this addiction, who do not know or do not understand it. No one notices, when the red line has been crossed. It is a creeping, deceptive process. After all, if you are behind this red line and know that you can't stay "without", there is no going back! You are addicted and you will stay addicted all your life long!

Programming

My friend and I had our first meeting when I was 15 years old. He was sympathetic to me and not entirely unknown, since in my family, alcohol always around. My parents liked to surrender themselves completely at the weekends, and so it was often very noisy in my home. Sometimes it was so noisy, that I got annoyed , because I couldn't sleep at night. I was constantly worried that something might happen, my stepfather would freak out and my mother could be harmed. I was constantly concerned for my mother.

By nature, I've always been a little "crybaby," but the weekly excesses in our living room also contributed to my fears. It wasn't generally the case, but often.

Since alcohol was considered completely normal in my family, I got to know it in the course of my young life. At some point, I knew exactly what he was doing to which people. Some in our family were left out and funnier by him, others aggressive. The first I felt quite funny, but with the aggression I had my problems, and fear has been omnipresent!

The weekend was coming again, and I secretly decided to start a self-experiment. I just wanted to know what the stuff was going to ignite with me, especially since I knew there would be another clash between my stepfather and my mother. Maybe I got more courage and could finally tell my "old man" the opinion. Unconsciously, I took on a great responsibility for my mother, because for me it was right and important to protect her. I couldn't bear it if she was hurt. Unfortunately, I just didn't have the courage to stand up to my stepfather. That's why I had to try it! Since I was only 15, but looked like 12, it was of course impossible to buy anything myself. I hired an older buddy to buy me a small bottle of cherry liqueur. I hid them in my room immediately after receipt. It was Friday night. I was really excited because I didn't know how to react to the liqueur and thought about a while, until I turned the bottle up quietly. Smell it for the first time. It smelled far away of cherry, much more was there the smell I already knew, that of alcohol! Should I drink or not? I first drank a very small sip and observed the effect that was triggered in me. A warm, pleasant feeling permeated my interior. Not bad, I thought, so just take another little sip. The pleasant feeling intensified. I didn't understand how it could make you aggressive, because I just thought it was wonderful. There was also a change in my head. This inexplicable, pleasant lightness flowed through me and since the liqueur did not cause me anything evil, I took another sip. Now I was doing really well, I listened to music and was very happy. At a late hour, the noise level in the living room rose. It was like a miracle, because for the first time I didn't care about the volume. I wasn't interested in what was going on between my parents. I listened to music, took a sip every now and then and rejoiced at the magic agent I had found. When the bottle was empty, I fell asleep contentedly. When I woke up the next morning, I noticed a strange taste, had a slight headache, could only partially remember the evening, but I knew that I had felt very comfortable and slept on top of that deep and firm. My mother called me for breakfast. It didn't taste like anything else to me. But I didn't notice anything and then I retired to my room. I had overcome my little "hangover" the next day, I was looking forward to the next weekend, because now I had found a real friend who protected me from my fear. My brain has been programmed so that when scary situations may occur, I only had to drink the relaxing liquid!

The Stranger in Me

After this first extraordinary experience I liked alcohol. As far as my budget allowed, I indulged myself every weekend, a small bottle of liqueur, sometimes two. My parents didn't know about it at first, but later, when they heard it, they couldn't prevent it. I started to like my new friend, almost to love. He did me good, gave me support and a new self-confidence, and above all he took away my fear. But without him, the fear was more or less present in me. Often it was unrealistic fears, that I simply couldn't defend myself against. Out of the blue I suddenly got panic, heartbreak, sweats, my neck was laced and I thought it was over. I often struggled with such symptoms – hard to describe what was going on in my head!

At the time, however, I thought it was a physical problem, I was terminally ill and would have to die soon. After a few years of extraordinary popularity with this drink, I could already tolerate a whole boot. I was proud of it and thought it was an enormous feat and a special talent. The small bottles became large; it wasn't just one day a week, and I started it more and more often in the early morning just before work. My apprenticeship as a cook was not exactly conducive to a serene handling of alcohol, because at that time, in many companies, drinking during working hours did not bother anyone very much. On the contrary, it was completely "normal".

My lifestyle was not without consequences. Sometimes in

the morning my bed was wet and I was lying in the middle of it, at night I fell asleep with a burning cigarette, or I was so drunk that I fell somewhere on it and hit my head, to name just a few. At parties I was always there until the end, had a big treat depending on the level and went home several times with a blue eye. My mother and sister were very worried about me. My mother in particular had a hard time and must have suffered a lot. Today I can understand a little what she felt when her son came home constantly drunk and always built some crap. She said very often that I was drinking too much, but at the time I dismissed it as ridiculous and belittled my problem. Sure, sometimes I tipped in a lot into myself, but everyone did. If you don't drink anything, you're a softie and who wanted to be that? I didn't, so I kept going.

When I was 18, I noticed for the first time that something was wrong with me and my drinking. One day I was sober and suddenly started shaking. Not like usual with the panic attacks, this time it was different. I was sweating, had irregular heartbeats and didn't know what was going on with me. Today I know they were the first withdrawal symptoms.

The next day I went to the doctor, who referred me to the psychiatrist. He asked some questions, including how much I drink. Every now and then, I said, he did not know the true extent. He then prescribed me sedative tablets (Faustan). I should take one or two of them whenever this strange restlessness appeared in me. I did the same and found that the tablets had a good effect.

After drinking the night before, I often felt very bad the next day. If there was no alcohol, I had to get something immediately. When the first sip ran through my throat and finally mixed with my blood, things went better again. Stupidly, sometimes, actually very often, it was not possible to get anything. Luckily, I now had the tablets. Since I am very keen to experiment, I took two tablets after a night out, the next morning and behold, I felt much better afterwards. No restlessness, hardly any trembling, good mood, and I didn't have to reach for the bottle again. That went well for a while, working throughout the day without alcohol, but with tablets. So I was able to survive the daily routine normally. As the evening approached, I felt an ever-increasing joy. Not for long, and I can enjoy the first sip, so my thoughts circled. At first I always started with beer, at the later hour there was liqueur or vermouth. I didn't care how the tablets worked together with the alcohol, I didn't feel any interaction, so I didn't mind taking alcohol and tablets at the same time. If I didn't have both, I was extremely deprived and could hardly take one step ahead of the other. It was hell to have to go to work like that. So it happened, that I sometimes, out of desperation, reached for cleaning products. Which contained alcohol. The stuff tasted awful, but I was able to keep me in the line for a short time. When I did such things, I wondered if I already had a mental disorder. I didn't know anyone who drank cleaning products, and I knew how dangerous it could be, but I did it anyhow.

When I looked at myself, I didn't recognize my personality. Who did I become? Had the alcohol made this stranger version of me, who does not care about the family, the work colleagues, the acquaintances, who were constantly entangled in lies? who was this man, that thinks only of himself?

My personality had completely changed. When others slept since a long time, I drifted around and broke into shops, always hoping to find money or alcohol. Sometimes I was successful. I was so fixated on alcohol that I even went to a church at night and ripped the sacrificial stick out of the wall. The 5 Mark (former german currency) I found in it, I immediately converted back into drinks. I was never caught in these actions, so I imagined in my already cracked brain that I was a master thief, and risked more and more. For my friend alcohol I did everything!

After a while, I was so broken that my mother broke my collar and she called me for detox. I would never have come up with this funny idea on my own, but my mother probably didn't find my way of life so healthy.

It was 1989. The first detox and at the same time the only one I could walk to. The ambulance or a good acquaintance was always on duty at all the following ones.

During the detox I recovered quite well. On the last day, the very young doctor told me during the visit, that I should never drink again, because I was an alcoholic! My thoughts were racing back and forth. At first I thought, he was kidding, but he was serious. Me and alcoholics? He's probably wrong, I convinced myself, he's just saying this, so I'm going to drink less. I agreed anyhow, left the detox station and did not touch a drop of alcohol for an entire year, but only for a single reason! I wanted to prove to everyone that I can be "without" and that I am not an alcoholic.

The 90s

At my one-year anniversary of being sober, it was clear to me, that now I could drink normally again, just like any other person. I didn't see why I should give up drinking alcohol.

The coming weekend was off work and that made me excited. On Friday afternoon I bought a bottle of vermouth after a long time. This should be enough to make the evening comfortable.

It was a weird feeling when I gave myself the first glass. It's like doing something forbidden. I thought of the doctor's words: "You must never drink again." I will prove that I have everything under control and do not have to drink after this bottle.

Let's go. Wonderful, the first sip made me feel incredibly well. Just as I remembered it! The warmth, the lightness, the good mood, everything was immediately back. I felt great. When the bottle was empty, I was back to the point where I stood a year ago. I couldn't and didn't want to stop drinking the next day, the weekend was still long, I wanted to enjoy it my way.

On Monday I came to work with still plenty of alcohol in my blood and hoped that no one would notice it. Of course my bad breath did not go unnoticed, but no one spoke to me about it. That gave me the boost to continue to drink. I went through this for a few days until I didn't care about the work and I didn't show up for the shift. I had a terribly bad conscience, but only until the first beer arrived in my brain. Then there is a second and third.

Now it was time to think about a strategy for getting out of this situation.

I went to the doctor, who of course immediately saw, what was going on with me, but luckily he handed a sick leave to me, through missed a warning from my work.

Another detox and again I stopped drinking. A few weeks went well, then again the same procedure. So step by step I became a quarterly drinker. It didn't bother me to get along for some time without my best friend, but then it grabbed me again, and I poured tons into me.

My mother eventually bought me an apartment because she could no longer bear my excessive lifestyle. As long as I was sober, I could cope well alone in my new home, but as soon as my brain screamed for the bottle again, there was only chaos in the flat. Regular contact with my family became less, I promised to stop drinking for good; unfortunately, I simply couldn't keep that promise.

During this time Martina and I got closer. We worked in the same company, seen each other very often and fell in love finally. She was a wonderful woman, had two children, and after a short time we moved together in a new flat.

I didn't stop drinking completely, but I was able to reduce it considerably for the first time. Martina knew about my exuberant drinking habits in the past, but just like me, she believed that they would no longer occur, because our love was stronger.

After just one year we got married. I now had a family, felt safe, loved my wife and liked my two stepsons. But after a while, the alcohol got more attention from me again.

I had now reached a new level. I drank every few months, but then so excessive, that I didn't care about everything around me, including my marriage. In one year, three detoxes sometimes took place in a hospital, in addition to the "cold withdrawals" at home. I was sacked for my job, and when I found something new again, it didn't take long, and I was back on the street. To top it all off, I discovered my passion for gambling in the casino. Sometimes I was there during the day, sometimes at night. With a number of excuses, I tried to justify myself to my wife, lied to her and almost drove us into ruin. I was constantly searching. It was a search for something that I couldn't find, but demanded my soul.

My way of life ruined my whole family. Martina cried a lot, got sick from my escapades and not only announced once, to end our marriage. The children suffered too, because they no longer had the family as they once were, who they wished and deserved. They were ashamed of their pals for their chaotic stepfather and I couldn't do anything about it. It was not uncommon for an ambulance car to stand in front of our house. Of course, this is always very embarrassing, especially for the children. Especially my larger stepson turned away from me more and more. Andy, my younger stepson, was a little more serenely, so I thought.

And another time I went to the hospital! Detoxification

again! What happened, weighed heavily on me. That's always been the case. It was only when I had torn up and destroyed everything, that I loved, that I came to my senses. What was wrong with me? I thought about, why I couldn't be a normal person. Nothing could lead me to repentance. Not even love! Why? I loved Martina very much. Nevertheless, I always promised, wanted to improve, to do everything differently, to be honest, to understand by now, that I am alcoholic, that I can never touch any alcohol again – but I did not get to grips with my addiction.

In 1996 I hit my worst low point. I was sober for a while after the last dropouts, had a new work and no craving for alcohol. I can't describe, what was going on in me at that time. Out of nowhere the disaster occurred. I became reckless, arrogant, started drinking and within a very short time, as so often, I destroyed everything, what I had laboriously built up before. I drank every day as if there was no tomorrow. One night I sat down in the car with a good amount of alcohol in me and wanted to experience something. I needed action. Somewhere there was definitely a party going on. Right before my destination: a traffic control! The officers let me blow with an result of 2.7 per mille. I handed them my car key and driver's license, the car was parked aside and I continued walking by foot. I didn't see all this so serious, it wasn't my first loss of the driver's license, and again it would continue, that were my thoughts.

Suddenly I realized that my appartement key was in the pocket of my jacket, that was in the car. I slowly sneaked back to the scene, looked around, saw no one and got into the car. After all of this, I couldn't feel like I was able to walk home now. I wanted to drive home. Said, done. The engine ran, radios volume I turned full on, and it started. I accelerated to 100 km/h, then I lost control.

Waking up in the hospital, i learned, that I had caused a serious accident, but I was incredibly lucky, because no one had been harmed. I only bruised my arm and some shards of the rear window were in my head. Not again, I thought. Now it's all over! I knew exactly what was going to happen to me. The license lost and so the job. Police, prosecutor, detox again, and – I couldn't remember, I was in tears.

This time I faced the divorce. That was the worst thing! How should I survive everything? Would I end up in the gutter now, without my wife's hold? I myself was to blame for this misery, why only did this insight come only now? Do you have to lose everything in order to come to good sense?

During my three-week detox at the Greifswald Odebrecht Foundation, my wife cleaned up the apartment. She had filed for divorce, and I had to live alone in a room because of the obligated year of separation. Separated from table and bed.

I went through the detox and came home. Luckily, all four of us were able to communicate normally, but reconciliation was unthinkable at that time.

I was sober!

I was sober for a very long time, more than 9 years! During this time Martina cancelled the divorce, I learned a new profession, then got a very good job, my relationship with the children got better and I was infinitely glad that the tide had turned again. We were generally doing well. Martina once said a sentence that I will never forget. I would be the best husband she could imagine if, yes, drinking wasn't. I too can say, she was the best woman for me!

I had (for now) ended my relationship with my deadly boyfriend, I didn't want to have anything to do with him anymore!

Old "love" rekindled

Some more than 9 years "dry", what an enormous achievement! But when I look back like that, I didn't find it that hard.

I remembered all the beautiful things: there was Martina, my wonderful wife, there were the children, I was able to expand my knowledge with the retraining in many areas, for 5 years I had a great job, a few years ago we built a house and to round off the happiness, a dog came to us. It all sounds a bit skewered, but I felt very comfortable with this life.

My memories recede and I ponder, whether there were any risky situations during my "dryness" in which I felt the urge for alcohol. Didn't exist! Of course there were sometimes thoughts, how it would be now, if I had a drink, but they were harmless, completely normal and not at all dangerous.

I can't avoid living completely without alcohol around me, so it's better to arrange for it. For the first two years of my "dryness" my dear wife did not drink alcohol, just in solidarity with me. That was very nice, but I didn't want her to have to restrict herself in any way, because after all, it wasn't she who had a problem with the deadly friend, but me.

As my thoughts circulated, I noticed that there were only the beautiful memories. Where were the terrible events, all the negative things that alcohol had done to me and thus also to my family, friends and acquaintances. Physical damage? Virtually none. I had chronic gastritis, which I have called my own since I was 18. The herniated discs? They didn't come from the drinking, and with my brain or mind everything was certainly fine.

But bad things happened!

I had abruptly quit at the time. 1996 was definitely the most disastrous year, but it wasn't just this one year. Through a chaotic year you don't lose everything, but at that time I had apparently lost everything. It is a creeping process that is not noticed until it is too late. One does not perceive the transition to dependency. I don't know anyone whose desire is to become an alcoholic. Still, there will be many. Why only? Nobody wants to experience these terrible events. The complete descent, the total isolation, the neglect, the "don't care" thinking, the worsening withdrawal symptoms, the enormous damage to the body – and often it ends fatally! Why do we do it anyway?

It is the intoxication that dwarfs all the negative things and makes them forget. Thoughts are focused exclusively on the intoxication, nothing and no one has room next to it. Nor- and I find this incredibly sad - human love.

Love for a human being can only help to pull oneself apart for a short time. After a few months, familiarity sets in, you don't find it so bad, when hurting your partner. It is believed that an apology and a bouquet of flowers are enough, to get everything right. Often it was just like that. But then you unconsciously become more reckless and think, what can happen when alcohol comes first again. She will forgive me again.

You don't realize that alcohol abuse is on the rise and you're doing things that you think are normal, but that are completely incomprehensible to others. There is the nightly drifting around, even though you are married, or driving by car in an alcoholic state. You think you have everything under control.

From 1982 on, alcohol defined me and my life. It was this constant frenzy that I had to get to the extreme. The escapades, the mental limitations, the criminal machinations, the loss of contact with the beloved family, all this is accepted, just to be with your friend alcohol!

But all these negative memories fade over the years and are barely perceptible at some point.

After this long period of abstinence, could I drink a glass again? It certainly wouldn't end that badly. Eventually I matured and knew full well, that I shouldn't overdo it. But even if I would be really cracking hard again, the next day I will be dirty, but this was only one day and then everything would be good again, I knew that.

Was I not an alcoholic in the end and had just had beaten a little too much over the strands? Sure, I've had a lot of detoxes, most in the hospital, but some also at home as a "cold" withdrawal. There were always a few "great" tablets, and with these the withdrawal was quite good to endure.

It didn't occur to me with this fantasy, how much I really had to deal with the detoxes and withdrawal symptoms, because I had lost my memories of them. Maybe it is also the case, that I can drink normally again because of my knowledge. I know exactly what's going on in my head. In the past, when I was drinking a lot, I didn't think about why I drink so much and why I couldn't stop until all was empty.

Today I know, how to behave correctly, if it's getting critical. I learned everything and heard it dozens of times. I was firmly convinced, that the more I knew about addiction, the less likely I was to slip in it again. Yes, I was even convinced, that I am not an alcoholic. I had to try it. I needed to prove, that I could control the addiction and not the other way around.

With these thoughts I brought my addiction memory to the awakening!

A great performance. Once again feeling that certain kind of nice, not having to think about anything, letting yourself go, giving in to the intoxication , – I could already feel it mentally, as it would be.

In the last few months I had done a lot of work. This intoxication was not to be despised, but it was completely different from alcohol.

Tonight, when the work is done, I'll take a good sip again, I thought. My brother Sebastian and I had opened a restaurant together. The concept was unique, the restaurant went very well. I stayed in the restaurant more and more often until next day, because it was usually very late and I just didn't have a need to go home in the evening. After work I was very often scribbled and it was better to stay there and not driving home. Sebastian lived in a small apartment, that belonged to the restaurant, and there were also another few rooms. One of them was our office, well equipped with sofa, table and armchair, perfect to stay there more often.

Only a small bottle, nobody notices and tomorrow there is nothing more, after all I am self-employed and have a pretty big responsibility.

From that moment on, a little more than nine years of abstinence were history! I had returned to my deadly friend!

Relaxation

Having given up my years of abstinence in 2006, I couldn't go back to that beautiful time. As much as I tried and as much as I wanted to, I couldn't do it. Every few months I got relapses, which were usually worse than the previous ones and sometimes even life-threatening.

At the moment, however, I was "dry" for a good year. My wife Martina and I had found each other quite well together again and lived a normal life. Luckily, she was still with me. I couldn't have blamed a separation on her after all, that she had experienced and gone through with me. How many times she had saved my life, without ever mentioning it. For them, it was simply self-evident. After all the chaos of the last years, insolvency, loss of the house, one year of separate apartments, moving to Berlin, then back to Rügen, constantly changing jobs, in between my failures – a miracle, that she was still there!

Now we both had our work again, were on a good wave, and nothing, but nothing at all pointed to a relapse. On the contrary, I thought, finally I have everything under control again. My goal: I wanted to top the nine years of abstinence. I had already managed a year!

A nice day began, I got up as always earlier than my wife, drank a cup of coffee, smoked three cigarettes, it was everything as usual. During this time I talked to my dog, whom I loved very much, and it was completely normal for me to have this conversation.

When I was really awake, the coffee and the cigarettes showed the expected effect, I grabbe my dog and walked her. I was looking forward to it. In my head, I had already thought about the way we were going to go.

On this walk, the sun was shining, the temperatures were mild and we walked 200 – 300 meters away from our block, to get to , where it was quieter and we could "let off steam". Again and again I met people I knew, and with whom I had a short but nice conversation. Then we were in that place. I let my dog Andra off the leash, we started to make our usual games and as always, we both had a lot of fun with it. I was really happy, when I saw that my dog was completely exuberant. The world was fine. I felt a total satisfaction, which then increased even in euphoria. No worries, no illnesses, life was a pleasure for me.

Suddenly the idea came out of nowhere, I should be able to amplify this euphoria somehow. It wasn't even the thought of alcohol just to keep that beautiful feeling in me and maybe increase it. The more I thought about it, the more an inexplicable nervousness spread in me.

Today I know, it was the so-called addictive pressure.

Gradually, the thought of alcohol came. This dangerous thought did not let me go. Attempts to make this idea disappear again were only a short-term success. I thought about the consequences, because I am an alcoholic and through my life experience I realized that "controlled drinking" is absolutely not possible.

We alcoholics know very well, that we are slithering back into disaster with the first glass. Nevertheless, I wiped away the supposedly negative thoughts, I didn't want to spoil the beautiful day and besides, I hadn't even drunk yet, so everything was fine. Still, it grabbed me more and more. I couldn't even concentrate on Andra anymore, just wanted to go home quickly. Along the way, I thought about how it would be best, to do something. Martina had to go to work around noon time. Once she was gone, I could get something. I knew, while I was coming up with this plan, that it wasn't right and it could end up bad again ... to divorce.

During my years of a drinkers career I had learned a lot, I was also aware, that I wouldn't stop it after one glass. But no matter, I pushed this thought far away from me and looked forward to this enormous relaxation that I would get, as soon, as the first glass would run down my throat.

Arriving at home, I became more and more restless and eagerly awaited my wife's departure. Surely she felt that I was different than usual. I couldn't fool her, she knew me better than any other person. Martina probably couldn't match, what was going through my head, couldn't she?

In the meantime, I got a bad conscience towards her and thought, what will happen, when she comes home tonight? Is it the final end of our marriage? She's been through so much with me, at some point she'll be at the end. I was close to tears as I thought how disappointed and sad she would be again, but the diabolical thought of giving me this beautiful, deceptive relaxation kept me in shackles. I talked to myself, after the first glass, I would see everything with different eyes and after the second anyway. Besides, I still had the opportunity not to do it, or just to drink only one glass and then stop again.

Finally it was time, my wife went to work, we said goodbye as always and I was kind of relieved, but still torn back and forth. Actually, I didn't want to drink and break everything as I have done so often. Then I thought again of the unique relaxation that I would feel, I just didn't want to give up on it. What should I do? How many times during my countless detoxes I had learned to take certain precautions when the pressure comes, for example, calling a familiar person to chat with him, drinking water until nothing fits in, biting into a chilli pepper, jogging, walking and so on. All this shot through my head. I was convinced that only the chili pepper would have helped me, but of course I didn't had that. So I had no choice but to implement my plan. I wanted it, I was almost obsessed, but I wasn't aware of it.

Fifty meters from our apartment was the Penny supermarket. First to Penny, I thought, maybe I'll decide against the liquor. Purely in the market, purposefully towards the liquor rack, and the quick grip to the bottle. I didn't have to think long, it had to be vodka. Add a bottle of Bitter lemon to mix, and off to the checkout.

Back home, I unpacked both bottles and put them on the kitchen table. I still had the choice, I thought, but – and every alcoholic knows that! I had no choice. When the first thought suddenly appeared this morning at the dog walk, from then on it was over with any chance of a choice! Hardly or not at all understandable for someone who is not familiar with this matter. How many times I've heard you just need the willpower, if you decide not to drink anymore, you don't have to do it, you just don't have a sense of responsibility, and how can you just do something like that over and over again, why don't you learn from your mistakes. Think of your health, think of your family.

All these accusations shot through my head at lightning speed, and I became angry with my fellow human beings. They had no idea about the alcohol, they thought maybe, I enjoy being an alcoholic and besides, this time it will certainly not be as bad as usual, I will be very careful and not let it get that far.

I turned the bottle up, I had already put the glass on, poured in, about two thirds full, if, then it should also look right, some bitter lemon on top, and the mix was ready. Andra watched me all the time. What did she think, if she knew what I was up to? I had no idea, I didn't stop at this thought for long, because otherwise, I would be sad again, now I wanted to put it behind me quickly. I took the first sip ...

It was early 2010. This year has been the worst thing in my life so far. For our marriage, it was the final end.

Serrahn

I was single for about two years and, after leaving my marriage, slipped deeper and deeper into the abyss, to short-term homelessness.

At first I had to deal quite well with my own business. Of course, I had to give it up soon for the loss of my driver's license. Now I saw no alternative to soak-up. My life was unstructured, there were no friends, and I reveled in self-pity all the time. Everyone was to blame for my disaster, but of course I wasn't.

The hospital was my second home, I let myself go more and more, had no more values, and my long-time addiction counselor was close to despair. She prophesied that I wouldn't live long if I didn't finally try to get out of this swamp. I didn't care, I thought, no one would ask about me anyway, besides, I don't have to worry about my worsening physical decay anymore. Constantly in the hospital, then again and again looking for something that I couldn't find.

It hung everything out of my neck, I didn't want any more, I was powerless, and my will to live was gone.

After a few days it was time again. With blue light I immediately came to the intensive care unit. I couldn't remember what had happened and why I was hanging on to so many hoses now. For my severe pain I got morphine at regular intervals. What a stuff! It relieved the pain and let me slip into beautiful dreams again and again. I was completely helpless, was fed artificially, a catheter took care of the rest.

When I opened my eyes for a short time, I saw my whole family sitting in front of the bed. Aha, so it's time, I thought, they're saying goodbye. I closed my eyes and, thanks to the morphine, floated over to the "magic forest".

After a week I was taken in a wheelchair to the examinations, a few days later I was able to walk on the rollator. I had severe pancreatic inflammation and great luck, said the treating doctor. I wouldn't survive any further alcohol excesses, as almost all the other organs were now severely damaged, he said. I wasn't particularly frightened by it, but then my "persistent" addiction counsellor persuaded me to undergo therapy in Serrahn.

In July 2012 I travelled with my belongings to Serrahn. Until then, I had never heard of this village. It was surprising to me, how beautifully located this little village was. Serrahn is located a few kilometers from Güstrow, directly on a lake, in the middle of nature, there are many animals, and the clinic was not bad either. Here I can endure it for a while, was my first thought. Luckily, I had a considerable supply of benzos (diazepam) with me. I just had to classify it well, then nothing can happen, because after all, it was about my alcoholism and not about the tablet problem.

The awakening came immediately after the first visit. As of now, no more benzos and to ensure this, regular urine checks were carried out. If they are positive twice, it would be the end for my therapy.

That was my end, I thought. A thousand thoughts shot through my head at the same time. I wanted to stop. But where should I go? I didn't expect anything good "outside". Nevertheless, I couldn't stay here either, since the cold turkey of my pill addition, i thought, I would not survive. I knew how difficult it was to withdraw. In the past, I had to get a few days without tablets, because I couldn't get them in time. That was hell! Now the complete removal of my beloved benzos? Unimaginable! For the first time I had enough and would continue to take them, that was my plan.

But I couldn't. I couldn't take the tablets longer, because I didn't want to risk being thrown out. I began to slowly assume that it must go without tablets! Perhaps this forced withdrawal will help me free myself from my drug addiction?

For me, the tablets never really caused a big problem, as long as I had any, it was more disastrous with the alcohol.

This withdrawal was the worst I've ever experienced! It was different, very different from alcohol withdrawal! With alcohol I had my experiences, after one, maybe two, maximum three weeks it goes up again. Now it was terrible. The nights were sleepless and riddled with hallucinations, at the day I didn't get one step ahead of the other. My esteemed roommate supported me wherever he could. I was very grateful for his help. Sometimes I thought, that's it, I can't get out of this turn, and I'll probably spend the rest of my life in the clap. The first time I was not even able to think about therapies, I could not even participate in the common meals. I was given a spasm protection, but that's it. It wasn't just once that I thought I was losing my mind. There were no clear thoughts left. I cursed the chief medical officer. What did this person do to me? Was he having fun seeing me suffer? Did he do any study, and I was the guinea pig? If I had been able, I would have been cut off, but I was no longer able to do that. Even after two months, I was still feeling very bad. I was particularly mentally ill.

The therapy was originally scheduled for 12 weeks, but in my case this was not possible, as I was far from having the withdrawal. I got one extension after another. Thank God!

After the 12 weeks, I hadn't thought it could be possible anymore, it started to go up very slowly. For the first time, I was able to focus on the things, that were scheduled for me according to the therapy plan. I recovered, even without tablets, and was glad that I was rid of this stuff. Now I liked the chief physician and thanked him.

I liked Serrahn. The clinic setting was very Christian. Every meal was prayed and thanked together, three times a week there was "biblical-oriented life support", the therapies were well balanced, and I felt very comfortable here.

Before Serrahn, I had almost nothing to do with Jesus. Here I recorded everything concerning the Bible and got to know him better. Especially the nice social pedagogue and the responsible sports therapist were a great help to me in Serrahn until the end, and not only with regard to Jesus Christ.

After 26 weeks, my therapy was officially finished. To my knowledge, it was pretty much the longest therapy ever undergone by a patient in Serrahn. For me, everything that has to do with alcohol and tablets was extreme, why not also an extremely long therapy ... This extensive time was simply necessary for me.

The social educator made sure that I came into the assisted living programm. Without this, I would have had to go back to Rügen. The premises of the assisted living were conveniently located right next to the clinic. So it was no problem to consult with the therapists when having questions. I felt home in Serrahn, got to know very nice people, among others Heinz Nitzsche and Pastor Uwe Holmer, the two had done great things and were founders of the Deaconic Center Serrahn.

In terms of health, I was well again, I was able to work through my accumulated penalty hours in the leisure home, there was nothing wrong with staying here for me. Christian charity was felt everywhere in this village. I found this very pleasant and tried to integrate myself into this community, which also worked very well. In May 2013, I was baptized finally .

Despite all the good experiences, the greed for alcohol gripped me again. Maybe I was doing too well and I couldn't handle that feeling yet. Maybe it was other reasons, or there was no reason and I just wanted to drink.

This was followed by the first detox in Güstrow, the time of the after clinic care was over and I moved to an apartment in Kuchelmiß, 2 kilometers away from Serrahn.

The Party

After Serrahn I was again for the third time to be in the KMG Klinikum Güstrow. A new, very modern, qualified detox station had recently been built there. The station F5! The staff was great, there were smaller therapie groups as well as one-on-one conversations, I always felt very well taken care of me there. Of course I preferred to see the hospital from the outside, but if I had to go in, then I was happy to be on the "the F5" . I was one of the first patients, so I was a "founding member".

During this detox I met Maren and Svantje. What have we laughed during this time! Both of them, like me, didn't take it quite as accurately at that time, with the never-drinking again. The girls had set up a small hidden depot on the hospital grounds, in which there were some bottles of "fun makers". In the evening we always visited this depot, and the two girls took a few sips. I was a coward in that relationship, but I found it quite funny.

Sure, we took part in the detox, for me it was also very violent at the beginning with the withdrawal, especially since I had problems again with the benzos, because I had started again consuming this after Serrahn. But after a while

I felt better, and I was able to deal with things that didn't really do me any good. But I didn't waste any thought on that. For me, all that mattered was being able to laugh again and have fun, the future was far away, and somehow it would continue anyway. But I also hoped, that I would not have to do any more detoxification, because this time it had gone to the hospital again with the "blue light", again the first time on the drip, again can no longer walk properly and again completely at the end. Actually, I didn't want all of this anymore, but who actually says, is notoriously uncertain.

The dismissal was getting closer and closer. During the detox I had to get a new apartment in Güstrow, because I had been kicked out of the old one. I liked Güstrow, just lived a few kilometers away and went to this town again and again, just to have a coffee somewhere and go back.

Funnily enough, I immediately got a nice new apartment without any problems. What luck, it could have gone differently, and I would have been homeless again.

In the last few weeks, the three of us had come closer, especially Maren and I. We made plans for what we would do, if we were back in "freedom." Definitely we wanted to visit each other. We were looking forward to it. After leaving the hospital, I moved into my new apartment. The first night was very quiet, everything was fine, but I felt that something was missing. I was in touch with Maren and we decided to celebrate something like a dismissal party with me. Svantje had to be there and Rolf, we also knew him from the hospital. Said, done and made preparations immediately. Maren and I first went to a super market, it was all supposed to be there. Also for the day after that event we had to have enough, because it wasn't possible that nothing was in the house the next morning. We were all very dependent and knew clearly, that it would not be just this one evening.

Arriving at my new home, we glowed in excitedness'. Ralf and Svantje would arrive a little later, and so we had the opportunity to get a little closer to each other. We both dealt with it very openly and were on the same wavelength. I was in love with Maren and knew, that she liked me a lot, too.

At some point we got really drunk. Svantje came and a short time later Rolf arrived. The party could begin. We filled our glasses, because at first we drank well behaved, later we didn't need any more glasses. The music ran in room volume. We talked and laughed a lot and the whole thing took its course.

Svantje's parents were always very worried about her daughter, didn't know where she was, what she was doing, if she was doing well, and that's why Svantje was in constant communication with her parents via mobile phone. At late night it became more and more fun with us. Maren and I looked at us in love, Rolf told us, what he had already experienced during his life, and Svantje was busy with her mobile phone. I had no idea what time it was, the music was getting louder, we were singing and screaming along and started dancing. Me with Maren, Rolf with himself and Svantje with her mobile phone. We decided, that everyone should sleep here, it was not complicated at all. I only had a slightly larger airbed, but finding a few blankets was no problem. But at that moment, there was no question about sleeping. We celebrated ourselves, made fun of how much the detox had once again had "success" with us, but also talked sensibly (as far as this 'reasonable' was still possible with us) about the people who had helped us a lot in the hospital, there were some of them.

There was the doctor, our dear social therapist, the very nice occupational therapist and the entire nursing staff, especially sister Julia. We drank to the good of the KMG clinic, to the people who gave us help.

Maren and I meanwhile cast "greedy" glances at each other, Rolf told of his erotic studio that he had recently set up at home, and Svantje rocked back and forth on her chair, holding her phone firmly in her hand. The doorbell rang. I asked myself, if there are still guests to come. We looked at each other inquiringly. Who can be that? I stood up slightly swaying, with my glass in my hand, and opened the door. In front of me were two policemen. I asked if they wanted to come in and celebrate with us. But the officials weren't joking.

It was about rest disturbance, the neighbours had complained, and we should make sure that the musics volume was set on normal level. I said that the neighbours shouldn't be so skewered, that we just had a reunion party. Apparently, however, it was seen differently. I kindly said goodbye to the policemen and promised that up from now we would be very calm. The music was quieter, and we chatted at a normal volume. It was now 4 o'clock at night. We enjoyed ourselves, no one really knew what he was drinking and where he was, but it didn't matter.

I must have nodded in briefly when the clattering of glasses and a violent noise scared me. Rolf wanted to go to the toilet, had supported himself at the table, probably a little too strong, at least the table overturned with everything that stood on him and broke into his individual parts. After a short second of shock, Maren and I started laughing very loud, because it just looked too cute, as Rolf lay between the rubble and the shards. He rappelled up, bled on his right hand and disappeared into the bathroom. Svantje crouched down in her chair and realized none of it. After a while Rolf came back. His hand was wrapped with a towel. Let's go on, he said, took a half-full bottle and drank it all in one sip. Well, hopefully that wasn't the last one, I thought. I panicked and thought feverishly about, where we would get something to drink now. Actually, what was bought should have been enough for at least the next day, but the next day had already begun. My panic thoughts quickly disappeared, somebody will get something, we all needed the replenishment. Maren and I sat close together and gave us looks in love. Rolf told about his massage chair, which was made by hand, because you could not buy something like that in a regular store. You would have to have relationships to get such furniture, nothing would be possible without it. But now, after a while,, he has everything together, the girls can come, and there's a whole lot standing on it, he said. Svantje woke up briefly, screamed that she loved her parents, and tipped off the chair quite violently. She lay completely twisted on the floor, her mobile phone in her hand, whining that someone should call her parents so that they knew, she was doing well. Rolf and I tried to put Svantje back in her chair, it was harder than we thought. The enormous amount of alcohol we had in our blood simply did not allow us to perform any reasonable movements. Rolf grabbed Svantje's arms from behind because he was the strongest of them all, lifted her up, but made a wrong move and flipped over. Svantje laid miserably whining under him and shouted that he should not rape her. Rolf wanted to rap himself up, clung to my sideboard and laid under the furniture. It was chaotic. I looked at the clock, it was just after seven. Not that the neighbors got upset again, because it was a bit louder and in the end the cops were back at the door! Fortunately, nothing happened.

Outside the day started and we could hardly kept our eyes open. Maren and I went to the bedroom, fell on the air bed and cuddled up to each other. We just wanted to sleep. Just before I sank into the land of dreams, I thought what a beautiful party, but it wasn't over yet.

A few hours later. I urgently had to go to the toilet, but could not assign, whether I dreamed or was up. I felt, that I sat down on the toilet and just wanted to do what I had to do, than I woke up. Luckily, but it wouldn't have been the first time I would make myself wet. I looked briefly at Maren, she was smiling quietly, but still asleep. Carefully, I tried to get up, that airbed wobbled back and forth, and it was a mystery to me how to continue sleeping. But she did. Quietly, I sneaked out of the room.

Man, did the shit go to me, and what time was it at all? First to the toilet, I could almost not hold it anymore. As I sat, I realized that everything was spinning, I had to take two benzos, so that I wouldn't get so much withdrawal. There was certainly nothing left to drink. When I thought about taking something alcoholic, I had to put all my strength into not vomiting in front of the toilet. When I was done and my stomach had calmed down a bit, I crawled around in my pants and found two more tablets. Thank the Lord, were my words, now everything is going to be good. By taking the benzos I felt at least for the a while being protected from getting cramps and delirium and would not get the big flutter. The thought alone drove sweat drops on my forehead. When I was "dry" from the alcohol, but had no benzos with me, it was sometimes like hell, and it was not uncommon for me to run to the nearest discount store in a sweaty bath and fetch a bottle. Strangely, the panic was gone immediately when I held the bottle in my hand, and I didn't even need to open it. The fear was gone at the same moment, it was weird. A vicious circle, I was on alcohol withdrawal, I needed the benzos, but there were no benzos and I panicked, I needed the liquid poison. "Unfortunately" I was so careless not to always have tablets with me, which was also very difficult to get these things from the family doctor. That's why I had three family doctors who all knew nothing about each other. Maren was also always totally keen on my "healing bringers", but she was still asleep and I didn't have to give anything away.

I had to find something edible now, just a little thing, because without it I couldn't smoke. That's why I've been overturned a couple of times, and I didn't want to risk that. In the fridge I found a ripped-up packet of cheese, took a slice and choked it down. It occurred to me that we hadn't eaten anything yesterday. For me it was normal, when I'm drinking, I have no appetite, but the others, well, no matter, I wanted to smoke one. I felt a small effect of the tablets and became calmer, sat down on a chair in the kitchen, lit one cigarette and started thinking slowly about where we would get supplies. The cigarette immediately gave my pulse a rather unpleasant effect, but I told myself that the tablets would immediately have their full effect, then it would be done again.

Maybe Rolf will go, or Rolf and I will go together to get a few bottles. Where was Rolf at all? And what about Svantje? I decided to smoke in peace and then take a look in the living room. I had strong memory gaps and tried to work through the night. There was the overturned sideboard, the broken table, the shards and, above all, what had happened to the other two? I feared the worst case. I was afraid to go into the living room, but I had to.

Let's go, maybe it wouldn't be as bad as I thought. I took a careful look into the room. It was worse than I thought. It looked like an explosion. Shards everywhere, broken furniture, tipping on the floor, burn holes, flower pots lay down, I didn't know where to look first. There, Svantje lay with her face on the floor wrapped in a blanket and, thank God, she slept. But where was Rolf? I couldn't find him. Maybe he was in the toilet, but I would have heard that? He was gone. I went cautiously so as not to step on the shards and tilts, quietly towards Svantje. She breathed a little weirdly, but she was breathing. Now she moved, turned a little bit in my direction and I thought, "my gosh" what happened to her face? The entire left side of her face was purple. My first thought was, if Rolf did beat her, but Rolf doesn't do that. Then I remembered that she had fallen off the chair, and this fall must have disfigured her face.

Suddenly I saw a bottle standing in front of the cupboard from the corner of my eye. I couldn't believe it, because if it was empty, I'd be pretty disappointed and certainly cry. Hallelujah, it was not empty, it was still three-quarters full. Today is my lucky day, I thought, took the bottle, immediately pulled me back into the kitchen and sat back on the chair.

The tablets worked long ago and a wave of relief passed me through. I was full of happiness. This will be another beautiful day, once my level is back in the normal range, I will be able to think clearly and we will make plans for the day together. Yes, the day will be beautiful, and tomorrow is far away. There will also be a solution for tomorrow. So, on life, on love, on happiness, what does the world cost! Now I just had to manage to drink without joking.

I took a cup out of the cupboard and filled it with water. When I drink the first sip, I have to drink water at lightning speed, otherwise the liquor in the high arc comes out again, because the taste at the beginning is totally disgusting. I did the same, and what a joy, everything remained in it. One more after. I was waiting for the effect, which quickly began. An incredibly beautiful, soothing warmth permeated my body, what a wonderful feeling, what an enormous relaxation. I let myself "fall" and thought, it's not all so bad with the alcohol, I just can't be totally drunk again and always have to make sure that tablets are available. Then nothing would happen to me, and I wouldn't have to go to the hospital any more. I was overcome with an undescriptive lightness. Another soothing sip, now I didn't even need to tip the water afterwards, it even "tasted" a bit. Cigarette on and take a few real moves, that didn't work with the first one, because then there was a cough and this vomit danger. The bottle was now just half full, and when the other two woke up, they needed something, we had to find a way to get supplies. Maybe there was something around somewhere?

Where was Rolf? I went back to the living room and looked around. Now it didn't seem so chaotic to me anymore. It was a lot broken, but if we had cleaned up and repaired some things, then it was definitely homely again. Svantje muttered something. I asked anxiously how she was doing. She said she would feel rellay bad. Once she sees her face, I thought, she would go nuts. I helped her to sit in the chair. The bedroom door opened and Maren came out. When she saw Svantje, there was a huge horror in her gaze. My goodness, what do you look like were her first words. Svantje, didn't understand what Maren talked about, and went to the bathroom. When a strange sound sounded, we knew she had looked in the mirror. Maren and I looked at each other and didn't know what to say. Svantje came back. When my parents see that, they will disinherit me, she said. I told her to sit down first, then we would drink something and make a plan.

I picked up the bottle and poured something in to everyone, now it was empty. We drank and remained silent. Svantje choked, I gave her something to drink, then she slowly got better. Maren had no major problems with withdrawal. So slowly our mood improved, mine was already quite good anyway because of the previous "pleasure". We were able to talk again and Svantje even laughed in between.

It rang. My first thought: The cops! Not quite as exhilarated as last night I went to the door and opened. What a joy, Rolf stood in front of me with two shopping bags in his hands. When he came in, he was greeted with a joyful hello from Maren and Svantje, because we immediately checked what was in the bags. He was our hero. In one second, our mood improved noticeably. The music was turned on and everyone was good. We made fun of Svantje's purple face and the neighbors.

No one was at zero per mille before the first sip. We all still had a considerable level. However, if we believe we are sober in the morning, the level is still well above zero. Nevertheless, we then have withdrawal symptoms because we "come down".

Not infrequently, when I was admitted to the hospital, a permille value between 3 and 4 was measured, in some cases even above 4. Hardly conceivable for someone who is not an alcoholic. Maren has already measured a value of 5.1. How such a petite person can achieve this high value, however, is obscure to me. A horrible state of affairs when you then slowly "drive down". Then I only have a single thought, where and how do I get something to eat now, so that I can feel better. With this thought, everything is completely hidden, the focus is then exclusively on alcohol. The body is literally screaming for the stuff, and everything else doesn't matter. There is no love, no friendship, no more behavior, and one comes, at least as I was, to the most oblique thoughts. From bottles of stealing in the discount store to aftershave and disinfectant drinking, everything was with me.

But I didn't want all these thoughts now. So there was a big sip, and the world was beautiful again.

It was around noon, we were in a really good mood, and so slowly we felt hungry. Nobody wanted to go out to buy something. I looked into my fridge. Except for a few slices of cheese and a glass of jam, there was nothing to find. We decided to call the pizza service, and in the meantime we could clean up.

We did it as best we could. We swept everything together, tried to put the furniture up, but it was more difficult than we thought. On the sideboard, 2 feet were broken off. Rolf had the ingenious idea of putting two empty bottles underneath. It worked quite well. It was now much higher on one side than on the other, but it was fixed. We immediately took a photo of our great construction because it looked kind of funny. There was nothing left at the table, it was total scrap. Luckily, I still had boxes that hadn't been unpacked yet. Two together, two on top of it, and our table was ready. We looked at our work, took a few more photos and were happy how well we had got it all. I was very happy, because after all it was my new apartment. The pizza could come.

Pizza service came a little later, and we started eating. Since we were all quite drunk again, I would almost call it food. Rolf was our frontrunner. Not only did he have half the pizza on his clothes, no, he had also distributed the pizza well in his face. But that didn't matter much to him, mainly something in his stomach, then you have a base again and can tip something on it, according to his opinion. Svantje meanwhile slightly twisted her eyes in different directions.

We opened up the third bottle and were happy that we had found each other. After some time there was nothing left of this third. Rolf had taken good precautions, and so there were two more in his bags. We got tired and all wanted to sleep a bit, so that we get fit again and get in party mood again in the evening. Good idea. Rolf and Svantje made themselves comfortable on blankets in the living room, Maren and I went to the bedroom and plump on the air bed. A little later we fell asleep.

Very slowly I opened my eyes, didn't know if it was morning or evening. It was dark, how long had I slept? My hand reached into the void. Maren was apparently already high. I tormented myself from the weird bed, took a while to think clearly, and then went into the living room from which I heard voices. All three were happily together and looked at me as if they were seeing me for the first time. I must have looked pretty wrinkled, because they started laughing at me. I went to the bathroom and looked in the mirror. It wasn't just Rolf who had handed out his pizza on his face. Washing my face would be good, actually it would better be a shower, but I felt too weak to do it now, I would do it if I was feel better a bit later. Back in the living room, I immediately needed a "mix." The bottle on the table was almost empty, I poured the rest with a bit of soda on it and drank the glass in one sip.

I had slept for just two hours, the others had got up about half an hour before me. The first was Maren. She had to refuel and woke up the other two. I asked anxiously in the round how much we still had. One bottle, Rolf said. Shit, so we had to go again. This time I couldn't get around it, this time I had to go, or at least go along. Everyone looked at how much money was left, we still had enough. The last bottle was "uncorked". I had quite a bit of a headache at first, but it quickly disappeared when I poured the second glass into me. Rolf and I put on our jackets and shoes, Rolf was barefoot, he couldn't find his socks. I saw that some of the pizza was lying on the floor and stuck to Rolf's feet. Clean now? No desire, we really wanted to get supplies, then we can still think about it, and besides, tomorrow is another day to do so.

We went to the Supermarket. On the way Rolf invited all the women we met to our party. Funnily enough, he couldn't convince anyone of this ingenious idea. I had to laugh all the time. Rolf didn't mind. We bought 10 bottles of vodka, 2 large cola and a packet of sausages. That should be enough not to get the big "flattering" for the next few days. We were still able to get something to eat, and in case of need, there was the pizza service. At the checkout Rolf made his usual jokes, fortunately I had a pleasant level, so nothing was embarrassing to me. I think the cashier was happy when we finally paid and left the market. Rolf said that when we were outside, we had to take a sip and smoke one. We did, and then we went back. I was looking forward to get home, especially for Maren. Maybe something is still going on today. The potency decreases significantly with increasing permille count, but this did not prevent me from drinking further. Anyhow something will go, I thought.

We were finally back. Maren and Svantje were eagerly waiting for us, they had nothing left to drink. We proudly presented one bottle after another. Great relief was felt. Nobody asked for something to eat, the Bockwurst disappeared without big words in the fridge. We all liked to drink vodka, on the one hand you get it down better than the clear, secondly, it has more percentages, which was always very important for us, at least as long as we had money. When the money was running out, it was not uncommon for me, to drink cheapest wine directly from the box . But this ended always in a disaster, because I got endless pain and had to vomit very often. I have this chronic gastric mucosa inflammation, when such drinks as wine came into my body, everything burned inside of me and finally broke out of me. But even that didn't stop me from doing it anyway, because I needed the alcohol.

Svantje's phone buzzed. It was her parents, who were understandably very worried. When Svantje was on the phone and had alcohol in her blood, she always gesticulated very strongly, from there it was no great surprise that she swept her full glass off the "table". What a mess, she screamed into the phone and then went to the bedroom. What she told her parents, we didn't know, nor did it matter to us. She came back, I had meanwhile wiped away the puddle with Rolf's sweater and put a filled glass on her again.

It rang again, it was the facility manager of my block, who gave me wordless a letter. I threw him somewhere in the corner and didn't worry at all, why I got a letter around this time. I wasn't even interested in who was the sender. We laughed, sang, drank, laughed, and the hours passed.

At some point, we all became calmer. Svantje slipped off the chair very slowly, climbed onto the laminate floor, managed to put on a blanket and immediately fell asleep. Rolf went to the bathroom and spent an eternity there. Maren and I kissed passionately and then went to the bedroom because we couldn't hold ourselves anymore.

Suddenly I saw a man standing in the doorway, looking through the room. Who was that? Maren and I immediately let go of each other and pulled the blanket over our bodies. The man left the room wordless and shaking his head, and we heard him talking to Svantje. She told him to wait in the car, she would come. On her last phone call in the bedroom, she had probably tried to explain to her father ,where she was. Apparently successful, because it was her father, who stood suddenly in my apartment. How did he get in? We hadn't heard any ringing. Svantje must have leaded him to my place, while he was still on the phone and then opened the door for him. He must have been terrified, when he saw his daughter. He then looked around the apartment. I could well imagine, that after seeing everything, he was in shock. What had his daughter gotten into! The apartment looked like a battlefield, and his daughter was completely disfigured in the face.

Svantje said goodbye to us, tried again and again to say that it was the best party she ever experienced, and then stumbled through the door. So she was up and away. We met after a long time. Of course on the F5.

Maren and I sat there in silence. Rolf, who was laying in the hallway, apparently hadn't realized the whole situation with him or he was so drunk, that he didn't care. He rolled to the side and fell asleep again.

My way led me into the living room, I needed something now. Maren came out of the shower and sat down with me. Our mood was depressed. By now it was already in the middle of the night. We heard a loud snoring from Rolf and grinned. Shortly thereafter, the snoring fell silent. Rolf tried to get up, making sounds that reminded us of grunt noises. We laughed, what was he doing? Then he tripped into the living room in his underpants and asked, who had just been with him. Either he had dreamed of it or he had hallucinations. Then he sat down on the chair and fell sideways at the same moment. Somehow he could grab a bottle, drank it, while laying down and immediately fell asleep again. Luckily, Maren was so insane to snatch the bottle from him that it didn't run out. A short time later, he woke up again.

You don't get a reasonable sleep anymore, if you are constantly drunk, wake up again and again quickly, because the permille number decreases and you have to refuel. Rolf wanted to pull himself up, but kept falling down, ripping along some half full bottles, which fell between my moving boxes. I didn't care, that my clothes and books got dirty, because the precious drink ran out. But actually there was still enough. Maren and I tried to put Rolf back on the chair, and at some point we even managed to do it. The party mood wasn't as great as the night before. Nevertheless, we were able to have a good conversation and had fun.

The next day we only spent drinking and sleeping. As we opened our eyes, we had to tip vodka into us. Sometimes it came out again in a high fountain, then another attempt, until it stayed in it. Then we drank and smoked and could hardly talk. Everyone was with their thoughts at the terrible withdrawal that awaited us. I didn't have tablets anymore, the liquor was almost empty. Besides that, Sunday was far away, and money was almost no more. I wondered where only all the cash had gone.

It was always like this, at the beginning there was enough of everything and after a few days: nothing more. I knew all this very well! This time, however, I decided not to go to the hospital. I knew, that if the withdrawal comes and I don't have any tablets, no more liquor, it can end badly. I have had seizures and delirium many times. Nevertheless, I did not want to go to the hospital again.

We still had so much that we could "survive" the night halfway.

According to an inspiration, I opened the letter that the facility manager had handed me. Let's see what was in it. I couldn't believe my eyes, I had to read it over and over again. That was the end. I showed him Maren while I was in tears. She, too, was completely stunned. It was the dismissal. I had to leave the apartment within 14 days and leave in a proper condition. I still had exactly ten days from today on. We hadn't seen how long we had been going through this scourge. I was completely missing a day.

I was just slightly drunk and understood what I was reading. How should I just do that? I had to talk to the caretaker the next day. Maybe there was another chance. Rolf said I shouldn't get ready, there's always a solution where there's a will, there's a way to go. I would have liked to have renounced his wise sayings now, he had a good talk, was not his apartment. Rolf had no apartment and lived most of his time on the street. So that was my way of doing it. We searched for all the liquor together and came up with almost two full bottles. They should take us through the night. When we had drunk everything, we managed to sleep all three.

When you get withdrawal, the nightmare begins when you wake up. While you are asleep, if you can sleep, you are very restless, but you are at least sleeping and dreaming. At some point you wake up and then the real nightmare begins.

The next morning. My first thought, no more liquor. Then the memory of the letter. I felt worse and worse from minute to minute. If only I had my medicine! But as much as I was looking, I found nothing, no liquor, no tablets. How was I supposed to survive this day, especially as I knew that I still had something in my blood and it was slowly fading. I drank water and smoked a cigarette, I didn't care if I would get dizzy. I already had sweats anyway. Who knows how long I could still smoke, because if I am fully on withdrawal later, I can only smoke a few pulls, and even these completely disrupt my circulation. In addition, the anxiety attacks, the tremors, the terrible thoughts, the sweating, maybe a seizure and delirium will come. It all went through my head. We knew, that the drug alcohol was a huge harm to us, over and over again! We also knew, that only with a complete abstinence, we could save our lives and steer it in a reasonable, perhaps even satisfied direction, yet our minds fooled us with the devilish illusion, that only alcohol is the real bringer of salvation!

Maren came into the kitchen. She felt also very bad. She mentioned, that she wanted to go home, than looked around and promised to help me cleaning up later. Now I was alone with Rolf, and I noticed how the withdrawal became strong and stronger. Rolf also left the apartment at some point, no idea where he wanted to go.

I was alone. What have we done? The best party, Svantje had said when she left. But it was as usual. The first few days were full of hits – and then? Then we only drank because our bodies demanded the poison. As long as there was enough, we weren't worried. But the "awakening" cannot be stopped. It always comes, mercilessly, mercilessly. I howled in front of me. The worst thing is, I already knew exactly what to expect on the first day, I knew that at some point everything would end in chaos. Why do we keep fooling ourselves? Why do we keep thinking, that we have everything under control, and why do we keep thinking, that this time it won't be that bad? This time we can do it. It's not possible, we never make it! As long as we do not renounce alcohol, we have to experience the withdrawal again and again.

Anyway. I knew, that if I go through it on my own now, it can be life-threatening for me. Even the doctors always advise, to never make a "cold withdrawal", because it could be the last. I knew all this, and nine more days until I loose my apartment.

A Star for a Day

This chapter describes one of my deliriums, which you can't actually describe. Nevertheless, I will try to give at least an approximate insight into the reality of an alcoholic during a cold withdrawal. It was one of the most impressive, concise experiences I've ever had!

Four days on withdrawal! No prospect of alcohol. It would have helped. But since I had no money and no more strength, I let it pass over me, hoping only a few more days, then it goes upwards again. Most of the time I lay on my airbed, without air. Every now and then I got up to find leftovers of tobacco crumbs, always hoping to "build" a cigarette from it. Every time I smoked, I thought my circulation was completely broken, but it didn't stop me.

Basically, I would have had to go to the hospital, everything would be checked permanently, the nurses come in every few minutes to see, if you are still alive. There are all sorts of drugs for this enormous, unwritable unrest. Above all, however, the hospital provides security. I was completely at the end, but I didn't take the phone, which at least would have brought the rescue to the hospital. I was ashamed, when I thought that the ambulance service would have to come back. In the meantime I was well known in Güstrow, especially with the paramedics and the policemen. I imagined what they would say or think, if they saw me in this pitiful state again. It would not be the first time, that all possible emergency services were standing in front of the house. And that would lead to have a crowd! No, I couldn't.

My thoughts wandered to the hospital, to the detox ward, where everyone knew me. I was almost even more afraid of the hospital itself than of the cold withdrawal. What will the nurse say, when I come again? It has just happened too often in the last three years.

I couldn't alert the ambulance service – I'd rather die here in the apartment, it doesn't look very good for me, anyway. Even if I came to the hospital, what would be after that? Is it all going all over again? Always the same cycle ... Drinking to the point of insensitivity, then completely slipping into the depths, ambulance, detoxification and thus recovery of the body (not the psyche!), then dismissal, and everything starts again. What a miserable life. This is not the first time I have shouted to God: Why don't you just let me go? Why do I have this disease? Why doesn't anyone help me? Where did my beautiful family life go?

An unbelievable anxiety attack filled me, I had to lie down again. Arriving on my "airbed," I just heard into myself, and I didn't hear anything good. This permanent restlessness broke me, then there were also the smaller cramps in the legs, where I immediately thought, now it's off, a seizure. I already had some behind me, within two of them, I had bitten my tongue during the attack. After waking up, my face and clothes were completely smeared with blood.

During a detox, I had noticed such a seizure in a patient. I will never forget this moment. A cruel sight. I didn't envy the people, who had seen me during my worst times, because every time it happened, there were people around me. Anyway, I thought, it is quite possible, that I also got seizures while I was alone. You don't know when such a seizure will come. It comes without warning. When you wake up, you don't know anything.

I wanted to die, but still had nothing more to fear than such a seizure, then I preferred to accept the delirium, although of course both can occur during withdrawal. In the hospital you get carbamazepine immediately and this at least protects you against these seizures, if you are lucky. Yes, in the hospital, but I wasn't there!

It started slowly, I knew, but it started. I first saw movements in the pictures hanging on the wall, in the curtains, and what else was moving before my eyes. Shapes or colors of objects changed that did not correspond to reality. Small animals came towards me that I had never seen in my life. They looked like beings from another world. Very impressive, I wasn't afraid. I admired the brain, what it could produce. Then the beings disappeared again. I smoked again, and this time my circulation didn't rebel as much as with the other cigarettes. Until that point, I knew I was heading for the delirium, but I hoped it would pass again, hoping I could fall asleep.

In one of my flower pots sat a small bird. I thought it came through the open window and made himself comfortable in the pot. At the same moment, I realized that the delirium was going to start. Fear rose in me. As long as I knew that the delirium could happen, the fear was absolutely there. It was real, it was tangible. But I was still hoping that it would pass, because when it came, I had to take precautions. This included locking the balcony door so far that I had no options to go out. I thought of everything. From the rope, which I wrapped around the heating through the balcony door handle and knotted so tightly that it seemed impossible to get out, to the barricading of the side door with blue garbage bags, which stood around me in large numbers, along with moving boxes, or with chairs. Hopefully I won't get it all during the madness anyway, because I lived on the 4th floor and that would be fatal! It is not uncommon for people who were in the delirium to think they could fly. The little bird in the flower pot was still there. I watched him and I heard him beeping clearly. Did he want to get out again?

(Here I have to say, that from that point on I was completely in the delirium, had no withdrawal symptoms and completely immersed myself in a non-existent world. I didn't experience the whole thing anymore, my reality was different now!)

I went to the window to help the bird out. But when I got there, it was gone. Well, I thought it made it to freedom. I lay down again, and it was there again. But now it began to transform, a cat suddenly sitting in the pot. I was happy, I wasn't alone anymore. I called and lured the cat to come to me. She didn't, she was probably busy with herself.

I didn't have any withdrawal symptoms anymore, luckily. Yes, I even felt relatively comfortable. Without shaking my whole body, I could get up and walk through the apartment. Plans ghosted through my head. Cigarettes had to be brought here, and more importantly, I had to call Maren, because I wanted to see her again.

Suddenly I heard voices and steps in my hallway. Yeah, Maren is here. But who was she talking to? I got up to check. Funny, there was no one there. The voices must have come out of the stairwell. I sat down again and thought. What had actually happened in the last few days? I didn't know, and I didn't care. Then again the steps and voices. That had to be her, I heard her talking to someone in my apartment. So back in the hallway, again no one there.

The phone, where was it? I looked around from my chair, walked through the apartment and finally found it in the bedroom. Of course, it was off and the battery was empty. Now I had to look for the charging cable, because without it nothing could be done. I found several charging cables, just not the right one. No matter, I picked up a few tobacco crumbs to roll a cig. After that, I would continue to search.

When I was smoking, it rang at the door. To my astonishment, no one was there when I opened the door. Was probably such a bell prank again. But it rang again. Since I was still in the hallway, I was able to open the apartment door quickly, but again no one there. I sat down on the chair and got a little tired. It was a weird fatigue. On the one hand, my eyes almost close, on the other hand I really wanted to know everything that was happening around me.

There was a party outside, I heard loud music and wanted to be there. It was this cool beat that I liked so much. I noticed that the song ran randomly and started over again and again. Suddenly I noticed it was my song. Yes, it was the song I wrote last time on the computer. How exciting is that! Out there in the world, my song was played. Finally it was time, finally I had made it with this song. With joy, I danced around the apartment, went to the balcony, wondered that everything was closed up there, and then decided to change to the window. I opened it and now I listened to my song very clearly. I shouted at people downstairs , asking them what this song was. But no one reacted. I sang along at the open window, after all I knew the lyrics.

It rang again at the apartment door. To my great surprise, Manja was in the doorway. I really liked her. But why was she here? I let her in and immediately told her about the song. I was thrilled. Manja too, she was happy with me (later I realized that she was just taking part in this game. It was just right and very professional, she probably had the experience and knew exactly what to do).

Super, I wasn't alone anymore, my song was still playing. Manja and I talked. Someone called at me from the outside. I went to the window to see who it was. The radio host from the house opposite, where there was a radio station, said I should come over, so that we could present the song together on the radio. My joy grew. I will be there right away, I answered him and went back to the room. I didn't know what to do first. Manja said I should calm down. Okay, I tried that. In the meantime, Maren was in the room, I hadn't even noticed, when she had come.

Maren was different from Manja. The two knew each other.

I liked both of them very much. When I asked Maren, what she thought of my song being played, she just asked if i was nuts, there wouldn't be a song. I was angry with her, why didn't she enjoy me success with me? Why wasn't she happy with me like Manja? Somehow she seemed annoyed. Why only? I kept trying to make it clear to her, how much that meant to me and that I would go straight over to the radio station. She screamed at me and told me to calm down again, but I didn't know what she meant.

Manja advised me to go to the bathroom first, because that wouldn't allow me to show up on the radio station. She was right and I gave myself a fresh up in the bathroom.

When I returned, three paramedics and a doctor were in the room. What do they want here, I thought. They spoke to me very calmly and just wanted to measure pulse and blood pressure. Why? I was fine, what was the point? After some back and forth, I got examined. Blood pressure normal, pulse normal, so, then they could go again. But they didn't go. The doctor said they had to take me to check on me. I started laughing and asked him if everything was okay in his head. Obviously I was in delirium, was his answer. Did he actually notice anything ? Sometimes you really wonder what's going on with the rescuers. Okay, they have saved my life a lot, I am infinitely grateful for that, but that really went a bit too far. I felt completely healthy, I could clearly think my best friends were there, and my song was still running.

I went to the window and told the radio host, that he should be a little patient, I had something to clarify here, then I would come over. He wanted to go on air with me right away, so I should hurry up, he called back. Why did Maren and Manja not say anything about it, on the contrary, they talked to me carefully and advised me to go along, it would be better for me.

Okay, they won for the moment, but I wanted to be back quickly, I can't let such a misunderstanding stop me.

Arriving at the ambulance car, I called again across the street to the radio host, who was standing behind the window, that I'm right back. There were people in the street cheering me on. What a feeling. I was finally a star!

We drove off, Maren drove behind us with her car. Once the ambulance car arrived at the hospital, I had to sit down in the waiting area of the emergency room. What a miracle, from the boxes of the waiting room ran my song. I was so excited. Looked around me and noticed that the people who were here didn't take notice of the song, for whatever reason. They were probably too preoccupied with their suffering, which I could understand. No one sits in the emergency room for no reason, except, of course, me.

Maren came in and sat down next to me wordlessly. I pointed them out to the music that was just playing on the radio. She said nothing. I asked her if she was happy about it? Suddenly, she freaked out completely unfounded, asked me if I was now completely crazy and had completely drunken away my mind. What was going on with her? We then had a pretty violent argument and she left the hospital. If only i am out here, I'm sure it's my turn and then everything will clear up. Hopefully my favorite doctor would be here, she would understand me. How many times she helped me in the past with detoxifications, how many times she talked to me about my very wide-ranging problems, she was a great doctor and was able to put herself exactly in the brain of a drinker.

I was called up, and what luck, my favorite doctor was waiting for me. In her office I heard my song again clearly. I looked at her joyfully and proudly said that it was my song. She liked it, examined me and wanted to keep me on the closed station for being well observed, as she said. That got me angry. I knew the "closed" through some previous stays in this hospital and under no circumstances wanted to stay here. She told me that I might have a heart attack, stroke or something like that because I was under severe stress. Why did she say such a thing? I wasn't stressed, but I felt so slowly that everyone had conspired against me. Yes, I had drunk the last time a lot, also had the first days of severe withdrawal at home, but now I was fine! From a medical point of view, she had to keep me here, but could not do so against my will.

Not against my will, that means to me, I could finally leave. Raised head I walked through the exit door, chatted with a few acquaintances at the smoking corner, said they had brought me in "by mistake" and went to the bus. Maren had given me some money, just before she left, so I could buy some cigarettes. She thought I had to stay there, but she was wrong.

I went to the bus stop and waited a few minutes to go home. On the bus, how could it be otherwise, the bus driver had set up exactly the station that was playing my song. I told everyone on the bus that I was the songwriter. Some looked at me strangely, others said nothing. Yes, it was already clear, I could understand them, how else should one behave when suddenly such a shooting star sits next to them on the bus.

Arriving at home, I leaned back in my chair. Then I thought about calling Maren. No, at first, I had to get over to the radio station as soon as possible, because too much time had already been lost due to my short hospital stay.

The phone rang, great, I thought, the radio sender was calling, but it was an acquaintance who just wanted to chat with me. How I feel, and what I do, whether I'm drinking and all that stuff. I immediately told her about the song that is now in the charts. She thought it was really cool and said she was so happy to know me. We talked for quite a while until I told her that I had to hang up because I still want to go over to the station.

I went to the other side of the street and unfortunately the presenter could not be seen at the window. What a bad luck, I thought and started checking the name plates at the front doors. Since I couldn't find anything, I rang here and there, knocked on the doors and asked the people, where is the radio station?

Suddenly, a few policemen stood around me.

Why they were there, a mystery, but there was no escape. At the end of the day, I was fixed and calm on the station I was so afraid of to be in. It was, as so often, the "closed".

You don't forget a delirium. Although it is a completely different, non-existent world, in which one finds himself, one sees this world as realistic in its very way. When it is over, you can still remember every detail. I can still remember every delirium until today. But this one was the most fascinating!

Shared suffering

It was something special. We no longer had a partnership, but we couldn't really leave each other. Again and again our paths crossed, mostly on the F5.

Maren was just looking for a flat, luckily, she finally got one in the same hallway where I lived. Our apartments were right opposite to each other. I was lucky to have found a domicile again after being thrown out of the previous apartment. This time I didn't want to spoil it again.

Maren moved in. Her home was perfectly furnished, unlike mine. I had no furniture, I just called a small table with chair, a few moving boxes, some blue bags and an airbed from which the air still kept escaping, my own. At Marens place, there was everything, that was supposed to be in a reasonable apartment. For this reason, the events almost always took place at hers.

During this time, my thoughts were constantly about alcohol.

As long as there was money, I was able to provide myself with the stuff quite well. The penny market was right next door, and mostly I managed to get my supplies there. The food was, as it has been for years, secondary. A dear acquaintance provided me with something edible every now and then, so that I did not face hunger. For me, the main thing was always to have high percentages in the house. After a short time I had no more cash, and then the big fluttering began. There were constant fears of procurement in my head.

During my free fall into the depths, it was always like that. On the 1st of the month the money came from the job center, my mood was exuberant, I bought and drunk, according to the motto "What does the world cost?" and somehow it will continue. After one, latest after two weeks, I was broke. I didn't care, if I had something to eat or not, the real disaster: no more liquor! If I was lucky, the money was enough for a few beers or cheap wine in paper boxes.

Now Maren and I lived on one floor. Often we were both on withdrawal at the same time. Maren didn't have it quite as hard as I did. At least she still managed to look reasonable. During this time I had no interest in my appearance, I didn't even get to brush my teeth. My clothes were either totally torn or so dirty that no normal person would put on such a thing. It is not uncommon for me to squeeze into a pair of Maren trousers, which even fitted me. It was like a nice side effect: hanging on the bottle for two weeks from morning to evening, eating nothing, I lost about 15 kilograms.

When we were really dirty in the morning, we took out all the empty bottles from the blue bags (they were all around us) and let them drip out one by one into a glass. Sometimes two 4 cl glasses came together. That was enough for the time being to think about, how we could get to have alcohol without money! After that, we looked for some tobacco crumbs, Maren stuffed a cigarette and we shared it. We shared everything! My tablets, the liquor, cigarettes, food, just everything. Two of them could be better endured.

After the first cigarette, our plan was fixed. It was the same every morning. We always found a few cents laying around somewhere. I tried to straighten my hairstyle halfway, put on a slightly thicker jacket and went either to the Penny or to the Sky Supermarket. It was hard for me to get down the stairs. The withdrawal was so strong that I thought, I couldn't make it back.

After an eternity I entered the market, put two buns in the basket and looked around trembling but methodically. My goal was the liquor rack. With just a few simple steps and moves, two bottles disappeared in my thick jacket. From there I went to the checkout. Sometimes I was particularly good, then also a box of cigarettes went into my pocket. The cashier didn't notice anything, and I was finally out again. Saved, I thought, and headed home, which was now easier and much easier. On the way I didn't grasp anything, it was enough to know that there was something in my bag!

When I came back, Maren saw my shining eyes and knew, it had worked again. Together with the cigarettes, a nice day could begin. Maren filled two glasses, we couldn't mix anymore, but we didn't care, we drank. As always at first big choking, sometimes we simmered right in the bucket next to the table, but with the second glass it was already better. The horrible withdrawal symptoms were initially averted, but we also knew that these two bottles could not get us through the day. They just made sure that we could cope and carry out the most necessary actions. But then we really did only the bare minimum.

By midday we had emptied two thirds of our bottles. We were doing reasonably well as a result. From now on, we had to think again about the supply. Once again Penny would have been too risky, only the Sky or Aldi remained. I was caught stealing at Aldi before, and if the boss was present, I would be taken out immediately, because he knew my face. All that remained was the Sky. There were wide aisles, and there was a chance for good vodka. I had to keep an eye on the sometimes present detective, then it could go well. This morning's fear had disappeared because of the alcohol level, and I set off. This time, too, I managed to bring home two bottles.

That's how it went day by day. We became brazen and started sometime in the morning. Maren didn't really want it, but let me came along. We were a good team, almost like Bonnie and Clyde. While distracting a saleswoman, Maren let two bottles slide into her handbag. It went so fast that even I sometimes didn't notice. Then it was my turn. It was not uncommon for us to leave the market with four bottles plus cigarettes.

But then times changed. We were getting worse and worse, despite the alcohol. No one of us was able to leave the house next morning. We shared the rest of the previous evening and drank in silence. We both knew, that detoxification would be inevitable, only when and how we couldn't see. Maren put on her glass and immediately scribbled in the bucket. There was nothing left in it. It also became more and more critical for me. I had just four tablets. We shared, everyone got two. Then it was over. The withdrawal symptoms went more and more severe. I feverishly thought about how we could get liquor.

Where was my friend? Why did he let me down? Why did he allow this calamity? Was he perhaps not my friend and had only in mind from the beginning to destroy me? Did I fall for him again and again and is his goal my death? I could not and did not want to deal with these appalling questions. I was getting worse and worse, and I would have done everything for a sip. My heart started to race, severe anxiety attacks came, more and more frequent, freezing and sweating alternated, and I had severe pain in my stomach, kidneys and esophagus everywhere. I imagined the alcohol going through my throat, the blood and finally my brain. Oh, how would that be nice now, but we had nothing left, and Maren vomited for the second time.

The penny market was about 100 meters away from us. There was the saving drink. I kept thinking about how I could make it there. But there was no solution! The walk to the toilet was already so strenuous, that it was impossible for me to leave the apartment. We had already betrayed the pizza service, because of this this, option no longer existed. So, no chance, we surrendered!

Maren lay crouched on the couch and barely spoke. My thoughts rotated. If a seizure or a delirium comes again? The fear grew stronger and could hardly be endured.

In the midst of this desperation, I got the ingenious idea of drinking the vomit bucket, which I did immediately. I choked down a considerable amount of it, feeling my esophagus was being blown up, and let myself fall into the armchair sweat-bathed. There was no question that there was some alcohol in this liquid, which now only had to work. One strangler chased the other, but I kept drinking all of it. Slowly a small effect was felt, and I calmed down a little.

Maren wept quietly. I haven't had any tears for a long time.

These would only flow into streams during the next detox.

Why are we just so scared and do it every time? Was it worth those few days we could spend in high spirits? Why did the insight always come, when we were absolutely at the end? Our organs were badly affected, and the brain probably did. Actually, we didn't want all of that. This constant torment. The perpetual procurement pressure. We didn't shy away from criminal activity just to calm our bodies. Again and again hospital, if only it would not be so damn hard to go this way of abstinence. I knew how to do it. How beautiful it is "without". But this road is so extraordinarily difficult! In the current situation, it seemed impossible to me! How could we ever find the right solution for us? Or was it long too late?

Suddenly, at some point at night, it rang. Did I have hallucinations now? No, it rang again. Maren slept, I dragged myself to the door. In front of me stood our buddy Klaus.

Was he the salvation...?

Stingapple and angel's trumpet

Klaus was there and I felt a relief. As he entered the living room, Maren muttered, "What does he want here?" Klaus sat down and crawled around in his bag. In my mind, I prayed that he would immediately pull out the saving drink. He did! My body was shaking with excitement as he turned up the bottle. Maren was suddenly awake when she heard the familiar crackling sound. I knew all this was just a delay from what will inevitably come, but it doesn't matter.

Klaus quickly mixed three glasses with the cola he brought with him. Carefully and with both hands, I stopped and let the drink run into my body. An enormous burden fell off me at that moment. Because of the mixture, I hardly had any stranglehold. Maren did the same, and her tears dried up.

A few glasses later we even managed to talk normally. Everything that Maren and I felt an hour ago was a thing of the past. I didn't see our cold withdrawal as dramatic as it had been just moments ago. The positive thoughts prevailed. All three of them thought about what to do next. Klaus suggested to go to his place, he had enough rooms so that we could sleep there with him. By taxi we went to the small village, he was living, next to Serrahn.

After we had gone through a few days again, we were finally at the end. To make it all worse, I was also on pill withdrawal. All three of us were somewhere in a corner, no one said anything. We would have had to go to the hospital urgently, but we lacked the strength. Klaus and I drank aftershave, which was only a short help. But it was enough to smoke a cigarette without circulatory collapse.

Klaus made his way into the kitchen. I didn't feel time anymore. What was he doing? He came back with two transparent plastic cans, in which there was something like tea. Angel's trumpet or stingapple, was his question to me. I had never taken anything like this before, but because I was so desperated, I wanted to try it, to see how it works. Perhaps the withdrawal will be mitigated. I choosed angels trompete. Klaus brewed a big jug with the stuff, which we drank. Maren declined. I thought, what's going to happen, it can't get any worse.

I noticed, that after a while we could talk to each other in a normal way, even make jokes. The angels trumpet seemed to have a good effect. I had no withdrawal symptoms and was happy, that Klaus had something like this in the house. I absolutely had to stock up on this. Then we tried his stingapple tea. I was getting better and better, and I couldn't get enough of it. Later we didn't bother to brew, but simply poured the dried leaves into a glass, cold water on it, and our drink was ready.

Suddenly there was a fox in the living room! Where did he come from? Klaus lived near the forest, and in between we had left open the front door, so the animal must have come in, I couldn't explain it to myself otherwise. We tried to scare him out, but he kept coming in through some corner. I walk you around the house, I heard myself telling the fox. Astonishingly, the fox obeyed me, and we marched off.

It was in the middle of the night. Every few meters a street lamp lit up until they were no longer there. Where was I and, above all, where was the fox? I saw a road sign: Ende Kuchelmiß, where Klaus lived, / Serrahn 2 kilometers. Ok, I was on the road towards Serrahn. I continued my way, alone, the fox was no longer seen, despite my loud shouting.

After some time I stood in front of the entrance sign of the village. What did I want here? It was dark and I couldn't explain what had brought me here. Then I came up with a good idea! I didn't want to go back to the boring road, so I continued my way across the field to take a considerable shortcut.

Immediately after a while I stood in front of a forest. I knew, if I only followed the river, I come back to Kuchelmiß.

The fox was back, and we moved together and continued to talk loudly. I told him my life story.

It was mid-October and I noticed, that the slats I was travelling with, only one was hanging from one of my feet. I must have lost the other one in the sticky field.

Suddenly I was standing in the middle of the undergrowth, I didn't know where I was. But I wanted to go on, back to Kuchelmiß, and fought my way through the scrub. No trace of fear, not even withdrawal symptoms. What a nice night. Despite my light clothing, T-shirt and jogging pants, the other slats I had also lost by now, I enjoyed my existence in the forest. I felt completely free, as if there were no problems, and trotted forward, singing funny songs.

Some time had passed, when I was unexpectedly standing at the edge of the forest. A field in front of me. Scattered lights in the distance. Was that Güstrow? I couldn't imagine, but what else should it be?

Back across the field, barefoot. Every now and then I slipped on the damp ground, but it didn't bother me much. I now had to know which "city" was in front of me. Progress was more difficult than I thought, and slowly the cold became noticeable.

After a felt eternity, I stood in front of a sign. Cuddly! How could that be? My night trip felt like I run 30 kilometers, and now I was back in Kuchelmiß. It was, after I did not want to go to Serrahn, my original goal, so, well received again!

The dawn set in, it slowly became bright. I quickly moved on to a slab building, because that was where Ina, a good acquaintance, lived, who I could ask for help. I rang her door. When she opened, she immediately slammed it back and told me to disappear. What was going on with her, I thought, but didn't dare ring again and moved from there. Outside, I thought about how to get to Güstrow to my apartment. In no second did I think of visiting Klaus and Maren. It was as if I didn't know where I was coming from.

Now I felt slowly emerging withdrawal symptoms again. It occurred to me that Kathi also lived here somewhere in the prefabricated buildings. After ringing the wrong people a few times, I was finally right. Kathi opened the door and looked at me with big eyes. Did I look so terrible? After she let me in, I barely recognized myself in the mirror. My appearance was worse than horrible! It was a miracle that she had opened the door for me. I was totally dirty, with no shoes, jogging pants and t-shirt almost completely torn, and I saw nothing familiar in my face. She gave me something to eat, a few clothes from her son and drove me to Güstrow without much words about it. I was very grateful from her doing that, and now I slowly realized what had actually happened.

We had replaced the strong withdrawal with Klaus by stingapple and angel's trumpet tea, but by that I also came to this trip, which was life-threatening in hindsight, because I had taken tons of this dried stuff to me.

Anything was right for me to escape the withdrawal symptoms! It didn't matter, whether it was life-threatening or not. Later I found out, why I was so much off the track during my night out.

There are alkaloids in both, in the sting apple as well as the angel's trumpet. These substances have an enormous effect on the psyche. During consumption, one loses the sense of time and gets strong hallucinations, which make all possible and impossible things seem real. Even small overdoses can be life-threatening or even fatal.

I would like to warn against ever considering taking these plants!

I had a guardian angel again, otherwise I couldn't explain why I was still alive!

I met Maren again during a later detox. She was a day patient and had probably finally got the turn. I indulged it to her from the heart. I didn't hear from Klaus anymore. Ina, my acquaintance, had to slam the door on this crazy morning, because she herself was affected and wanted to protect herself by this action, which is completely understandable to me. Perhaps that is what I would have done in this situation.

Whether the fox was real or not is still withdrawing from my knowledge.

No permanent residence

I had "done it"! After the predictable ejection from my second apartment in Güstrow, I stood on the street. Until now, it had always gone someway, but now? What should I do?

Just released from detox, I was standing in front of the hospital and had absolutely no plan. The apartment was vacated, my clothes packed somewhere in cardboard boxes, my friend had taken me to the penultimate stage quite gradually and without my consent. The last one was probably death!

Luckily, it was the beginning of the month and there was still money. Physically I'm not going to be bad this time. After a detox, the "addiction pressure" is particularly high, especially when, like me at the moment, you are facing nothingness.

I knew exactly where my path was going to take me. Now everything didn't matter anyway, so I can also ball the pear again, so this horrible situation can definitely be endured better. I bought two bottles of clear liquid and cigarettes at Aldi and sat down at the bus stop. One bottle disappeared into the travel bag, the other into the jacket.

After a few minutes I saw my situation as not so bleak, because he was back, my friend and comforter. He brought hope and courage, perhaps I had done him wrong when I cursed him. It is not that bad, quite the contrary. He gave me the strength I needed now.

It's summer, and I can sleep outside. I became more and more cheerful because I thought I was going to visit a buddy.

When the bus came, I had emptied the first bottle and was good. I will not let myself be subdued, nor am I alive!

For the first few days without a permanent residence, I slept with my buddy. He, like me, had made friends with alcohol, and we got along well. During the day I was always somewhere and met people I could drink with. I had to pick up my mail from a professional caring person, but it often happened that I didn't went to him as agreed, he had to call me all the time, and I was sometimes untraceable. That, of course, caused trouble. When I had appointments at the job centre or at the court, I always had alcohol in my blood, because without it, was absolutely not possible. Before, I only drank so much that I still managed to talk to some extent. I thought no one noticed anything – today I'm sure everyone knew, what was going on with me!

Then came the times when the money was running out. At the municipal table I got something to eat, but the problem of alcohol procurement remained. I already had enough experience with it and applied it in the tried and tested style. Theft, every day! Out of ten cases, at least one went wrong, so I was constantly dealing with the police and always had any criminal charges on the cheek.

It was not uncommon for me to drag myself into the discount store in the morning with last strength, go to the shelf, turn up some bottle and drink out in the middle of the market. I didn't care who watched, because my body was screaming for the poison! After that I sometimes had to go to the "catacombs" of the supermarket and answer to the servant. Most of the time, the police were also called in. I was banned from the house one after another and soon I didn't know where to go. Because even though I had money, I was not allowed to approach the markets.

Sometimes I didn't know where to sleep. The seasons could not be stopped, and it became cold. In some houses you could get in without ringing. There I slept in cellars on cardboard boxes or, if I was very lucky, on a blanket. The fear, that I was caught was omnipresent. In the morning I sneaked out quietly and set out looking for alcohol and something to eat.

At that time, everything tasted good to me. Discarded, half-eaten kebab, which were certainly laying around for a few days, I took and ate. I searched in paper baskets, found a liquor bottle from time to time, containing a few centiliters of the saving drink, and poured it greedily into me. Occasionally I had a seizure in public, lay in my excrement somewhere, either the emergency services or the police gathered me and took me to the KMG hospital. There I woke up, generally stayed only a few days, dismissed myself against medical advice and was back on the street.

Meanwhile, I looked more and more repulsive, but I wasn't particularly interested. Basically, I was just waiting for death!

Then there was another unexpected climax, through which my friend, finally, became my deadly friend.

There was a small party in a village just outside Güstrow. With a buddy in the apartment. By this time I had just received money and was also well stocked with my much-loved tablets. We were four and knew each other from the detox. A dear acquaintance drove me to the said village.

During the ride I took a few sips and one or two tablets every now and then. So I got out of the car in a good mood, and the party could start...

From that point on, all I know is, that all of a sudden there was police and paramedics. Then the lights went out with me in the truest sense of the word.

"Your name, call your name", "What day is today", "When were you born"?

Who just screamed at me like that? Where was I? I painstakingly opened my eyes with a flickering gaze to close them immediately. Bright light dazzled me. Then again, these intrusive questions. I wanted to say something, but no word came out of my mouth. I tried to get up, but then I noticed that I was strapped. Hospital, ok, but what was going on? Why was I here? Around me, these devices beeped, displaying heart rates, blood pressure, etc. From time to time I heard an irregular beeping. I slowly got my eyes up and saw a doctor in front of me, who lit up my face with a small lamp. Then again, these annoying questions. Barely audible, I answered what I knew. My name and birthday came to mind, but I couldn't talk. I hung on all sorts of tubes that I already knew, but still didn't know what had happened. The doctor enlightened me. I had been carried lifeless from the apartment, resuscitation and taken by helicopter to a hospital.

Reanimated? Helicopter? Why did they "take me back"? I was almost angry with the people, who had saved my life for the hundredth time. I didn't want to live! I slumped inwardly. Sure, it has always been my wish to fly by helicopter, but not in this way, especially since I hadn't been aware of it.

Now I lay strapped in a bed, supplied by meds and loving people took care of me.

I was in tears. For everyone else, my life was more important than myself. I screamed inwardly and silently for help, I cried for my mother, for my siblings, but no one heard me. Why couldn't anyone help me? Where was God? Why did he not help me, he could not make me suffer like this as a loving God! I prayed for my own death, but the prayer was not answered. I was torn, broken, bitter and hated myself abysmally.

Where was the freedom that my friend had given me? A freedom that had always been so indescribably beautiful. Relaxation, lightness, inner peace and balance? None of this was left. On the contrary, there were instead numerous hospital stays, detoxifications, rescue operations, intensive care, closed station, the fixations and so on... How many more times could I jump from death by God's grace? How many times have I been lonely, helpless, in pitiful conditions, closer to death than to life!

My friend put me in shackles where it was impossible for me to tear them! Was I just too stupid to realize, what he was actually up to me to do? Or is it nothing to do with intellect? Was it the circumstances, experiences, disappointments and fears that contributed to my intimidation? How should I ever find my way back to a normal life? Again and again the same question! I was guilty of the answer.

I still didn't really realize I had to do something. There was enough help, but I didn't use it.

The whole thing happened in April 2016, shortly after my 49th birthday. I was sure: I will not experience the 50th.

The F5 station

December 5, 2016!

With sirens I came to the CMM. As far as I remember, I had fallen down the stairs with my buddy completely drunk, after which he alerted the ambulance.

I immediately came to the "closed". I didn't want to go there, but my will was uninteresting at the time. A short time later, I was in the surveillance room. Was it so bad again that I had to be monitored? I couldn't get away with it, the station was heavily secured. These thoughts were too exhausting for me, and since there was still enough alcohol in my blood, I fell asleep hanging from tubes. A restless night followed, because I came down! This was terrible, because the permille number had to have a certain value until it is safe to administer medication for the restlessness. Drinking water a lot, I was told again and again. I drank and drank with trembling hands. The whole body hurt, especially my face. In addition, the restlessness, this constant heartbreak, I was already on the verge of madness again. Then finally the tablets, against the cramps, and distraining. I greedily swallowed the stuff and waited for the effect, which I hardly noticed at first. Nevertheless, I was under medical supervision, which gave a little bit of security.

I dropped into bed. For hours I stared at the walls. Sometimes the pictures hanging there moved, I immediately panicked because I thought a delirium was on the way. My breathing was heavy, and I bent over in pain, because my organs were no longer the healthiest. At regular intervals, a nurse looked in. I waited longingly and impatiently for the next dose.

The tablets were available every two hours in the first time. My sense of time had disappeared, but then the door opened again and the nurse handed me a small cup with the medications in it. After that I tried to sleep a little, but this turned out to be impossible. My thoughts were wrong, and so I continued to stare at the wall and watch the pictures.

The next morning I was washed, put in a wheelchair and driven to the CT. I couldn't walk alone. In the elevator I saw my mirror image and hardly recognized myself. One half of his face was completely swollen and had taken on all the colours, the other looked not better and was yellow. Couldn't trust my eyes. I had the usual hospital garb on and because of my pain I suspected that other parts of my body were also badly affected.

After the CT we went back to the surveillance room. During the day it was not quite as creepy as at night, because there was a lot of confusion of voices on the station, the door opened more often, it was a visit, the food was brought, and time passed faster. To sleep was unthinkable, and I knew from experience that it would need quietness a while.

After a few days I was able to move on the rollator, and a little later it started again without any aids.

Then finally I came to the F5. Thank God! The staff of the "Closed" is consistently sweet, nice and competent. But the F5 was my familiar station. I knew all the nurses and staff, I knew the social therapist, the doctor and all the other therapists since the opening of this station and they knew me. There have been a number of stays I have spent here so far.

I was assigned a room, a twin room. I was relieved, maybe I finally managed to sleep. The first days I didn't have to participate in the therapies and could also eat the meals in the room. With my fellow patient it was a good get-through, I slowly became calmer inside. But there were these thoughts, how long will the detox take, and what about it? Will my family know where I am and do they care? What's next for me? Should I go through tablet detox? Will someone visit me? I envied my fellow patients who was visited every day, but it hadn't been the case for me. A few months ago, during a hospital stay, I had received an unexpected visit from my (step) son Andy and his girlfriend Meike. The joy was huge, hardly writable. Especially since I hadn't seen Andy for an eternity and didn't know his girlfriend yet. However, I struggled with my emotions and had to be careful not to cry during the entire visiting period.

This time I didn't get a visit, maybe it's better, because it wouldn't be easy for my visitors and for me. My sense of shame was back, and I looked horrible. A nurse told me that my skin looked like that of an old man. Of course, I didn't see it that way, because for me the skin was completely normal. But maybe I already had a twisted perception of things.

Again and again I tried to push away these torturous

thoughts, but to no avail. It will take me a long time to get back to normal, if anything else can be saved with me.

Then I finally got a little better every day. After consultation with the ward doctor, I decided to carry out the withdrawal of tablets in parallel. I knew what was coming, but I was able to stay in the hospital longer, because nothing good was waiting for me outside. The benzos should be "sneaked out", every few days the dose was reduced. I was able to live with this detox, because I was in control. The problem for me – and when I thought about it, I panicked – was, that the tablet level continued to drop and then my anxiety returned. Because originally I had been prescribed these tablets for panic and anxiety. On the other hand, I still had enough in my blood, didn't need to worry about it for the time being and was able to concentrate on alcohol detoxification.

My body recovered, I could even laugh in between. With each detox, there is at least one patient who makes everyone laugh with his sayings. Many of us knew each other. Most of them weren't there for the first time, so after a few days there, we had more or less funny conversations. It was almost always about alcohol. We all had an intimate love affair with this chatter and knew exactly how much it hurts us, but that didn't stop us from making jokes about our deadly friend. It happened that we were so amused by our consumption that the on-duty sister had to remind us that we were on a detox station. At this point, however, I think we needed this gallows humor. It helped us to forget our own miserable situation in the short term. We were all sad figures, had to do with our physical withdrawal, partly a catastrophic path behind us and we were happy that we could laugh again. We all had something in common, our friend, the alcohol.

For me, the tablet reduction was done "covertly", which means that I did not know how much milligrams the dose was reduced. But I felt the change. As a result, the symptoms I knew from the past slowly returned. There was again the feeling of insecurity, the balance disturbances, restlessness, lack of pleasure, lack of motivation, low heart rate and sweating in simple activities. I couldn't walk up or down just some stairs on my own. Crossing roads or walking in the morning as part of the detox became enormous burdens, which often took the courage away from me. Sometimes I considered throwing everything in and going back to the old corked life.

I got exceptional help from all the staff of the F5! The conversations with the excellent social therapist and the very competent ward doctor gave me courage again and again. The nurses and care staff did an excellent job, approached me and never made me feel like I was a scrapped alcoholic. On the contrary, on this station we were all regarded as normal people and treated in the same way. Among other things, the responsible occupational therapist made sure that we were allowed to cook or bake something beautiful every week, and we were never stigmatized by anyone for what we had done in the state of being drunk. I felt safe and understood on this station. However, I still cannot explain where these dear people get their motivation from! They see the same picture of us over and over again, they know that only a few manage to stay "dry" over a longer period of time; and yet they are always kind, friendly, show compassion, and above all, they do not condemn us!

After four weeks of my stay, a woman was admitted, who, like me at the beginning, was completely on the ground. I didn't know her. The first days she was understandably barely visible, because she struggled with herself to be able to walk straight again. After a few days she came out of her room and sat next to me in the sofa corner. She put a Bible on the table, and I looked at her in complete amazement. Then she said, smiling, that she believed in Jesus Christ!

From that moment on, my life changed!

For the first time on this station, I felt that something was different than usual. Suddenly I felt like I didn't have to do any more detox on this station. I couldn't explain where that feeling came from, but it intensified to the end.

Her name was Verena, and she knew a lot about Jesus. From that point on, I completed my prescribed walks, which I had to take in the morning and evening around the hospital grounds, together with Verena. We told each other about our horrible lives and talked a lot about the Bible.

In Serrahn I had already learned a lot about Jesus, but unfortunately I had not taken it so seriously later. Now everything was alive again in me, and I found new courage to cope with what was coming to me.

The social therapist of the F5 had managed to organize a shelter place for me in Ribnitz-Damgarten. I wasn't particularly enthusiastic about this idea, but I had only one alternative, and it was being without residence! So I agreed with that proposal. A week later I had thought about it again and wanted to go to another facility, where long-term therapy would have been possible.

For the first time I saw the usually very quiet, mastered and nice social therapist "Calm down"! Resting may be a bit exaggerated, but she was visibly angry with me and insisted on my therapy in Ribnitz-Damgarten with her unreputable arguments! Because I liked her and didn't want to expose myself to her "anger," I agreed with a heavy heart.

How grateful I am to her today, that she has not deviated from her line! Sometimes other people know better what is good for us and what is not, because they simply have an expanded perspective.

When I made my way to Ribnitz-Damgarten, I had this strange feeling that something completely new was going to affect my life!

I never saw Verena again. I am also infinitely grateful to her, for she has rekindled the love for Jesus Christ in me!

Ribnitz-Damgarten

Here should I live now? In this village?

I only knew the small town from passing through. If my favorite football club Hansa Rostock had a home game, we drove from Rügen to Rostock and then had to go through Ribnitz-Damgarten. It was back in the 90s when Hansa was still playing in the Bundesliga. I found nothing special about this city, somehow it always seemed very barren and bleak to me.

Actually, I didn't care where I was. There had been no family contacts for years, my family had long turned away from me. It was self-protection for them, which I understood. How many times I had promised: "This time it was really the last time, this time I stop, forever". I had always disappointed her, and unfortunately I often didn't care what my siblings, my mother, or even my then-wife thought or felt. As long as I was in the "tea", the alcohol was the first priority, and nothing and no one had a seat next to it. Not even the family. At some point I learned that it would be best for my loved ones if I were to go on it. Sounds violent, but from today's point of view I can understand it. This constant fear of having to answer a call with the death message ... this constant fear of where his son or brother was and how he was doing. Especially for my mother, my siblings and my wife, the years of my drinking must have been their absolute horror. When I think about it like that, I can't imagine how you can deal with something like that. It seems to me to be terrible, horrible, unacceptable. But, as I mentioned, I didn't worry about it during my excesses. Addiction is probably stronger than love!?

Well, I was in Ribnitz-Damgarten. It was clear to me, one month only, and then I disappear from there. Back to Güstrow, I will get an apartment, this has worked many times. If the caregiver is to take care of himself, he gets money for it. In any case, I am not staying here!

Since I was better off, the KMG had done a good job again, the arrogance, ignorance and arrogance in me increased significantly again. How did they want to help me here, I wondered. Like many therapists, I had already bitten their teeth, to no avail. In Ribnitz-Damgarten, of all places, should the big "breakthrough" come? It was just ridiculous. No one could help me anymore! Since I had no contact with Verena anymore, I did not take it so precisely (for that time) with the Bible.

Sandhufef 1, what a nice name for a long-term facility. (That was the address.) In this institution were men and women, who could no longer get their lives on their own. Just like me. For a long time it was no longer possible for me to live independently, which is, why I had been assigned a supervisor by the court for a few years. I thought it was very practical. My caregiver took care of everything, whether finances, health insurance, my criminal history, just everything. So I was able to sit back. Most of them here had a criminal career, so it wasn't anything out of the ordinary, I didn't have to be ashamed.

My sense of shame had disappeared deep in the basement anyway. I arrived here with a half-shredded travel bag and a cloth bag from Aldi, which contained everything I owned. My ID card was signed with "No permanent Residence", and when you have that address, you don't expect much of your life anymore. Some clothes I had received from a nice fellow patient at the last hospital stay in Güstrow, some I still had myself. It wasn't much, but it had the advantage that I was quickly finished unpacking.

The whole house was shown to me right at the beginning. Since there was no room available, I had to stay in the conference room for the first time. In the small room there was a fold-out bed, table, chairs, a closet and – what luck! – a TV and even a DVD player. Great, I thought, then it doesn't get quite so boring in the evening. I didn't know anyone here, and this room was a good retreat for me.

Luckily, I still had my phone. This was not self-evident, because in the past I had mostly only owned a mobile phone for a short time. Either I had lost it or it was stolen, or I had sold it well below value to get cash for drinks in return. Now it was still there, and I had halfway in touch with the outside world, and by that I don't just mean Facebook.

I hung around a lot on my phone for the first time, and in between I regretted myself. What kind of miserable life did I have? Actually, I was lucky that I was still alive, instead I was whining and howling in front of myself, of course only when I was alone.

Sometimes I remembered the Bible, and I listened to sermons on Youtube out of boredom.

In this institution, work therapy was the first priority. However, there were also other forms of therapy, such as occupational therapy, sports or relaxation. All this was not strange to me, because it was not the first facility in which I was given shelter. There were about 40 inhabitants in the house "Confidence". The residents were divided into four groups, each with a therapist. I came into group 2. There was still a lot of potential in this group, and we had a very good main therapist.

There were quite a few residents who were mentally restricted by alcohol. Many here had the so-called Korsakov syndrome. This is a form of dementia, usually caused by excessive alcohol consumption. It was terrifying. I had never heard of this disease before, although I had already had a lot going through in terms of such special facilities. It was not immediately apparent to the residents who were concerned. It was only when they knew them longer and closer, that it became clear that some pieces of the puzzle were missing from the brain. I was and still am shaken by this disease. At the same time, however, it is infinitely grateful that it has not hit me (so far).

After a few days I was assigned to the kitchen. There was a well-furnished in-house kitchen, I am a chef by profession and I was looking forward to my work therapy. In this field I met Jeanette. We worked together in a team. From the beginning we were on a wave and were able to talk to each other quite unbiasedly. That was very good for me, because I now had a person to whom I could tell a lot about myself.

Jeanette had been here for a few months longer, was happy about my arrival, and we spent a lot of time together, even outside of our therapy. In the evening, I continued to listen to the sermons and was now able to distinguish which Bible teachers were good for me and which did not.

So slowly it became a little more pleasant and relaxed in Ribnitz-Damgarten.

The first four weeks you are not allowed to leave the place, which is common practice. I am probably the only one who was happy about it, because I had not lost my fear and panic. Outside the facility, I couldn't imagine myself to be. For years, everything was all about either alcohol or tablets. But I shouldn't take both. I was still quite broken mentally and couldn't imagine that would ever change. Inside the house I felt safe, never went outside. Hence the joy of the curfew. A helper accompanied me to go shopping, which had to be from time to time. It worked out quite well, since I stayed close to him and felt safe.

Now at some point the four weeks were over, then luckily I had Jeanette when it came to shopping. From now on it became difficult for me to attend the doctor's appointments alone. The first four weeks I had been driven. That was easy, but now?

I used my old tactics, which have been "proven" for years. When an appointment was due, I said to myself before going out: if I get panic attacks, there is always the possibility to go to a shop, buy a bottle and drink. As a result, the panic would have disappeared immediately. In recent years, this method had worked well. I knew that With this tactic I would risk a lot, so it should be the absolute last resort in Ribnitz, so only if I was about to collapse.

I never needed my crazy strategy against panic, thank God, never to use it during my time in Sandhufe 1.

At the facility, selected "candidates" were tested for drugs at irregular intervals. It also affected me because I was addicted to meds, too. And indeed, the result was positive. It came as no surprise to me, because I had never stopped taking illicit medication (benzodiazepines), I had only reduced the dose.

My psyche was programmed to make me think that if I don't take at least a little bit of this stuff, I wouldn't survive.

The consequence of the positive result: another four weeks curfew, a conversation with my therapist, attempts to explain in the group, appointments with addiction counselling, but the worst, I finally had to stop the meds if I didn't want to risk being thrown out.

It was a disaster for me. Nobody here knew that I was still secretly taking the tablets. I had kept it a secret from the beginning. And now? Without it? Inconceivable for me, it was hard enough to get a grip on that with alcohol. Very quickly, thoughts grew to leave the facility.

That's always been the case with me – if any difficulties occurred, I immediately considered fleeing. But in the meantime I liked it quite well here, so I had to find a way.

I left the tablets away for two days out of fear of further testing. Physically, I had no problems, but psychologically. I knew that, and I knew it was going to happen. What should I do? I thought back and forth, but then decided to talk to Jeanette about it. However, my trust in other people was so badly damaged that it was not easy for me. Eventually I talked to her. I knew she wouldn't be able to help me much in this matter, but I had to talk to someone about my secret. I told her the whole story that despite the detox I never really got clean, where I got the tablets from and where my problem was. She listened attentively and gave me some advises. With her I was also able to hide my tablets, because a room search was to expect.

When I left her room, I was relieved. It was just talking that helped me. Jeanette could chat very persistently, but she could also listen. I appreciate that in her. My confidence grew.

My problem was still there, but I didn't see it quite so stubbornly anymore. On the contrary, all or nothing, I told myself and continued to take a small dose of the benzos every evening. I've had enough of it and they'll be enough for a while. I took only a fraction (1/8) of the usual amount and hoped that it was not visible during the quick test. My bill went up. I sweat blood and water every time I test, but I was always lucky.

The conversation with my therapist went so far quite well. I showed honest remorse, and it was really remorseful! However, I couldn't help but lie to them. I am still sorry today because she had a sincere interest in helping me. But what should I have done? Telling the truth? Then there would have been an ejection or another withdrawal of tablets, and I never wanted to do that again.

I just couldn't talk to her about how much I was still tied up by this tablet addiction, I would have liked to have done it, but I knew the consequences. It was clearly set out in this institution for me. No medications I depended on! So I moved on a very narrow ridge.

On the one hand I had a very good standing here, was respected and beloved, on the other hand there was a bad conscience towards all therapists, especially since I was very well aware that I had to escape into these lies. I reassured myself again and again by arguing that I was here primarily because of my alcohol problem.

The 50th birthday. Until recently, for all who knew me, including myself, it had not been expected that this day would happen. But on April 20, 2017, the time had actually come. It was the most beautiful birthday of my life!

Sometime before, there were still very restrained contacts with my family, especially with my brothers. After a long time we had very nice phone calls again, I learned through them, how the family was doing, and I was glad that they started to take me back.

A few weeks before the 50th there was another conversation like this. My youngest brother Philip did very mysteriously, told me, that I should not do anything that day, but did not answer any further questions from me. Well, I thought maybe he would come to visit me, but I didn't expect anything.

That day was approaching, and I was thinking more and more about what might happen. I was terribly afraid that a drug test would be called for before, that it would be positive and that I would get a curfew again.

Then it was so far, I was excited! I had a day off and didn't want to go to breakfast. Congratulations from all sides have always been a little uncomfortable for me, but I had to go through that now. Luckily, it was limited. Many of my roommates didn't know I had my birthday today. Then I retreated to my room and started checking things on my phone.

At some point it knocked. My heart was pounding. Jeanette stood at the door. She beamed all over her face, took a step to the side, and my brother Philip stood before me. I was close to tears! We hadn't seen each other for four years. But that was far from all. Gradually my brother Sebastian, my sister Andrea, my niece Lorraine with her young son and ... it broke out of me in streams, my mother in the room. They were all there, I was crying like I hadn't done for a long time, this time finally with joy. I couldn't believe it, after almost five years I could hug everyone.

I was shaking, looking at everyone and being so excited that I saw the people I loved the most. I had guessed that my younger brother might have visited me, but that everyone was there, I never expected. How did they all get it? The brothers live in Berlin, my sister, my mother and my niece live with the little one on the island Rügen. Great, just great, wonderful! Oh yes, they had brought gifts, all things that I was very happy about and that I could use well. But without question no material gift could give me as much joy and happiness as the presence of these six people who were in my room today!

After the tears dried, I showed my family the house "confidence". I was as exuberant as I hadn't been for a long time. We then went to the sailing port together, ate delicious lunch, walked around, told, laughed and rejoiced at the reunion. In the afternoon there was still a nice ice cream, a joint photo was taken, and then this day slowly came to an end. We said goodbye warmly and were looking forward to the next reunion. This would be already in two months. Sebastian's 40th birthday. This is followed by my mother's 70th and in September the wedding of my little brother Philip was on. One reunion after another. I was just happy. After all these years, contact again! I felt a little like "the prodigal son" from the Gospel of Luke.

I thanked God for this wonderful day and gave my life to Jesus Christ! This time with an honest heart and with full conviction that I am simply not able to lead my life on a good path. He should take it for me, and he did!

After the drug incident, I was advised to contact the local addiction counsellor and a psychologist. I didn't know what it was going to bring to me, but I did. There were regular appointments with an addiction counsellor and a little later also with a psychologist. Contrary to my expectation, both the addiction counselor and my psychologist were a big asset to me. Especially the psychologist I valued was able to do things that I never thought possible. Maybe, it was because I opened up to her completely. In previous meetings with therapists or psychologists, I kept a lot secret and ultimately did not accept the help I was offered. This time it was different, everything here in Ribnitz-Damgarten was different, I didn't recognize myself.

Then a little shock! Jeanette has tested positive for THC. I knew she was taking crack every now and then, but I didn't worry much about it. As a back of this incident, Jeanette decided to leave the facility shortly. That made me very sad, because we had been getting closer and closer in recent times, and it was more than friendship. In addition, we harmonized very well with each other in our kitchen work area, I was worried about who might replace her. No one could!

Life went on, as they say. I was now quite a half year in Sandhufe 1, had a really good relationship with my roommates as well as with most therapists and with the head of this institution. I was in constant contact with Jeanette, and we were a couple for a while, but found that it was better for us to have a friendly relationship.

In Ribnitz, our intern founded a group of Alcoholics Anonymous, Jeanette and I were among the members of the first hour. Every Wednesday we met there, to talk about problems. A little later, other people were also affected, so that we are now a really good group.

My panic attacks went better. In certain situations, however, they were present. Sure, I could now go to appointments alone, but sometimes I came back sweat-bathed. Despite my small dose of benzo, which I still took daily.

In our facility there were a lot of bicycles. How glad I would have loved to ride a bike again. I hadn't done that for a number of years. Here it was a good time to drive quickly from A to B, especially since Ribnitz-Damgarten is a beautiful city and has a lot to offer. For me, it was unlikely to ever turn this into reality, because if I only thought about swinging myself on the bike, I already got sweats. So I quickly put those thoughts aside. I ousted them because I didn't want to burden myself with anything like that.

Now I have been in psychological treatment for a long time, where I also addressed the fear of cycling. My psychologist was so on that she always gave me some tasks until the next appointment, which at first seemed insoluble to me. Every time I went back from an appointment, I was on the one hand nicely relaxed, on the other hand I was really worried about how I could get the tasks I could do without lying to them. I had no choice, I had to do all the exercises. At some point there was also the task of cycling. I never do that, I thought. This time, she clearly demanded too much from me.

I was faced with a problem. This task was solvable and quite easy if I increased my tablet dose. However, this thought did not have a place in my brain for long, because that was out of the question.

I spoke to my group and work therapist about my "enormous" exercise. After these discussions, our work therapist agreed to do this task with me. In their presence, I got on a bike for the first time since I was at school. There was no muscle on my body that wasn't shaking. I tried not to let anything happen to me and carefully made a round on the yard. I hadn't forgotten it, but due to the great tension it was difficult to maintain that balance. That's enough for today, I thought, and I was happy to have taken the first step. The next day we drove a slightly longer distance together, about 200 meters. Gradually the distance became greater, sometimes through the forest, sometimes on a dirt road and then even over the road. We always drove close together so she could intervene in an emergency, giving me the security I needed.

It got better and better, I had to be careful not to be reckless and to remain attentive despite my euphoria.

When cycling trips were announced as part of the sports therapy, I was there. My feeling of life increased, because I got a bit of freedom by driving and was now able to free myself from these panic shackles. I had help, very good help from our work therapist and I took advantage of this help, without which I was in any way uncomfortable.

My self-confidence grew, and I didn't find it bad anymore that I had my domicile in Sandhufe 1. On the contrary, I liked it here, and I could almost imagine staying in Ribnitz-Damgarten. I saw my psychologist's responsibilities as challenges, which I mastered with regard to fear, and noticed that I was changing.

At some point I spoke to the head of long-term therapy, and we realized that we are both Christians. I couldn't believe it, because I had prayed a lot for finding Christians in Ribnitz-Damgarten. She recommended Christian events, which I liked to attend.

After Jeanette's departure, I worked with the "red Zora" in

the kitchen – the lady specifically asked that I call her that in this book. After some initial difficulties, we harmonized very well together. She is also a chef by profession, was able to bake very well, and so we complemented each other. I cooked a lot, she baked almost every day and tried new creations that tasted very good. It was fun, we laughed a lot, and we were given a free hand in the kitchen. It was a sign of confidence on the part of our therapists. They knew we were relying on us.

I've been in the facility for nine months now, I've had a physical fitness that's acceptable to me again, and mentally it's getting better and better. There was almost nothing left of the half-dead wreck, the pitiful, unteachable man that existed in me a year ago.

In the last two or three months I have been looking more and more often towards "outside". Every now and then I met with people outside the facility to pursue common interests. I did it not out of compulsion, but because it was good for me. We had our group of Alcoholics Anonymous. Once a week I visited my Christian house; when herbs or mushroom walks were offered, I was there, and so "doors" gradually opened, where I never thought they existed at all. I met people I really appreciate because they also helped me find the way that I am going today.

So slowly I got to a point of making preparations to leave the facility in the foreseeable future. For the first time, I seriously thought about it. I didn't want to rush anything, I was fine here, and when I go out, everything around me should be right. I knew how dangerous it can be for me in "freedom" and how many preparations would be needed to be able to live independently, contentedly abstinently. It won't be easy, but I thought about it, and by now it had to be Ribnitz-Damgarten! During my time here, I explored the city, discovered so many beautiful things in it, and now I love it.

During a herbal consultation I met Kristin. We got closer, and within a very short time she was my friend. I was with her as often as I could. We had common interests, understood each other very well and would have preferred to move together. However, this presupposed that I had to end my therapy prematurely, which we both did not want. Everything should be completed in peace and on schedule. This required patience, which I had already acquired quite well here in all these months. From my point of view, it would not have been so good to move together immediately. My gut instinct in this regard told me that restraint is the better way to do this.

I went looking for a home, had some help by my supervisor, contacted the job center and did everything I could to start a new life. Kristin gave me support on many things and was a great help. Despite the new situation, I did not let my therapy grind.

Apart from the apartment, everything went very well and smoothly in terms of my preparations. It is difficult for us alcoholics to get an apartment. This is because we do not have a particularly good past and at the time of our search we do not have the most prestigious address for a housing search.

That was the point in my case. After a few rejections, however, a caretaker finally found a flat for me, and so I got an apartment with which I am very satisfied and in which I feel comfortable.

The closer the time of the exodus came, the more fear crept into me. What if I can't do it again? Well, I had Kristin who gave me support, but in a way I needed her to maintain my abstinence, and that didn't work. I didn't want to be dependent on a human being anymore. In the past, this had been the case far too often, and there was never anything good coming out of it. So it was important for me to have my own independence. Only in my opinion is it possible to master the everyday dangers of life.

After all, everything was optimally prepared, the conversations with my therapist, my psychologist and also in my new circle of acquaintances encouraged me, besides, I could not live in the Sandhufe 1 forever.

With a queasy feeling, when the day had come, I moved out.

Due to the relationship with Kristin, it was not a problem for the first time. Sometimes we lived in her place, sometimes in mine. Our days were well filled, I had a lot of appointments in the first few weeks, was convinced to get work and couldn't complain.

Then the relationship broke down. I found that we did not fit together as well as we initially thought.

If you only maintain a relationship not to be alone or lonely, I don't think it's the right way to go. Sooner or later, you become more and more dissatisfied and ultimately unhappy. This, in turn, carries the risk of drinking again. I had to be aware of all the things that could jeopardize my "dryness". It was better for me to make my way alone for that time.

But now I had this unsure feeling again. Living alone for the first time. Do I get a good daily structure for me?

With my work I had imagined it too easy, I thought I could get off to a full start after seven years without work. But it wasn't that simple. On the one hand, I am very severely physically restricted, as I realized after an internship. The many years of drinking have left their mark, I have to accept it and live with it, especially since it could have hit me worse. On the other hand, you are not hired at any company if you write in your CV that you have spent the last four years in hospitals or in therapy facilities.

How should I fill out my day now? Would I get bored? My concerns were certainly not unfounded, because from my experience I knew, that one is very quickly unmotivated by boredom and can fall into apathy, which in turn leads to a "no matter what mood", and then the handle to the bottle is not far. So we must be extremely vigilant!

I have been living alone for a few months now and cannot complain about boredom. Somehow I have managed to do something, and I am very happy to do so. My days are well filled and I live a happy life. Of course, I also have difficult situations or times, usually only a few hours in which I am depressed. Fortunately, I have learned to accept these situations. It is important to recognize that these times pass, that they are normal and belong to life. Nor am I immune from pain or disease. On the contrary, since I have been abstinent, I have more pain than ever before in my life. My "friend" has left me a severe physical disruption. But it can also be lived with. I am in good medical treatment, I take a few tablets every day because I can't do it anymore without, and I get on well with it.

Anyone affected by this diabolical addiction must find his way. The road can be rocky and difficult. Perhaps some radical changes in living conditions are necessary for some. I know that we struggle to accept help and do not like change. However, both should come first before it is too late! Without help and without change, it is almost impossible to walk a "dry" path permanently. For some, as I have been, a complete replacement of the social environment helps, a change of location, and I would like to advise anyone who is so deep in the ... like me at the time, he is going to get involved in a follow-up facility. There you take the time you need to take part in all the therapeutic offers, even if some therapies seem at first glance completely pointless, gradually creating a new environment, which includes leaving the facility sometimes, not burying oneself in self-pity and taking with them all the conversations that exist.

I hadn't done all this for years – what came out of it, I tried in the previous chapters to describe in detail. It is very helpful to rediscover things we loved before our addiction, our skills and our hobbies. Unfortunately, these have been lost in the years of the drinking. For many of us, long-term therapy is necessary. During this long time, one has the opportunity to find themselves, to recognize themselves and above all to take care of themselves as one is.

We should no longer stick to old ideas or patterns and let bitterness makes us disappearing from our hearts! Let us walk with patience on a new path that is indescribably more beautiful than the one behind us! Let us not think of the past, but let us set out! Not everyone has the same starting conditions and not everyone can consistently leave their environment, but in Germany we get an enormous amount of help in every addiction-related life situation, we just need to accept them. Everyone takes a different path, but the main thing is that this path leads to satisfied abstinence.

I have found my confidence in the Christian faith. The foundation stone for this was laid in Serrahn. After that I had another four difficult years, until Verena led me back to Jesus during my last detox in Güstrow in 2016. But I really accepted my Lord only in Ribnitz-Damgarten. After all these terrible years without a way out, I believe that no human force would have been able to lead me away from alcohol. Only God could! I am very happy to go down this path with him and can't imagine anything else. He pulled me out of the swamp and gave me a new life, so it is my duty and at the same time an honour for me to nurture, care for and, above all, to keep out of alcohol.

During my therapy in Ribnitz everything fit together well and intertwined. First and foremost were the very good therapists, the addiction counselling, my psychologist, my roommates and also the people I met here. All of them, without exception, have contributed to my journey and strengthened me. I have been constantly looking for confirmation throughout my life and trying to be someone else. For the first time, I don't need it anymore and I finally realized who I am.

Since December 2016 I am "dry" and have found the "missing picture" in my soul. The "missing image" is Jesus Christ!

My Family

I was the first of four children to be born. Our sibling clan consists of my sister Andrea, my brother Sebastian, the "little one" Philipp and me. Sometimes our opinions drift apart, yet the four of us are very closely connected. There is almost two years of age difference between Andrea and me, so we spent our entire childhood together. Sebastian and I are ten years apart, Philip is seventeen years younger than me.

For me, my mother is the mother of all mothers. Even in difficult times, she has always cared for the four of us sensitively and long-sufferingly, protecting and supporting us. I have always known her as a hard-working, responsible and committed mother who still works in a regular way at retirement age. As a family, we experienced many and beautiful events together, which I remember very fondly. I also had a good relationship with my stepfather, except for the mentioned trouble.

Our mother was and still is the head of the family and always held the strings in her hand. From my point of view today, I can say that I had a pleasant and beautiful childhood!

My biological father died when I was seven years old. Through this break-up of a parent, my mother, but also Andrea and me, came up with challenging times.

It is incomprehensible to me how much my mother must have suffered as a result of my recurring escapades. How drastically I hurt her and my siblings. How many times has the hope died for them that I will finally become a person who will get his life on his own. There were a lot of situations that seemed hopeless, but my mother took me out of them. She always had the expectation that I would manage to go a sensible way. Unfortunately, I have not been able to meet these expectations over a long period of time.

At some point, they all had to turn away from me. I couldn't understand why no one wanted to have anything to do with me anymore. Today I know their behavior was right and the only way to protect themselves from me. I am infinitely glad and grateful that my mother, my siblings and many other family members have forgiven me and that I will not be showered with reproaches. In this case, too, it is an honor and duty for me to maintain this relationship!

From 1992 I had my own family, which, apart from myself, consisted of my wife and two children, which Martina brought with her into the marriage. The two boys were 10 and 6 years old. At first we had a lot of joy, but through my love of alcohol I destroyed the love for my family. My dropouts were not conducive to the children, and finally my eldest (step-)son turned away from me for understandable reasons. My wife Martina has suffered many times during the marriage, whenever we both thought, now it is going up, I tore down the building within a very short time. This eventually led to the divorce. I have had regular and cordial contact with Andy, my youngest (step-)son, for about two years, thanks to the Lord Jesus!

I know that I can never do well and unrequited what I have done to you over the years, but I ask for your forgiveness!

Thoughts on addiction

We know for about 50 years that alcoholism is a disease. In the course of our lives, certain circumstances can promote this disease and eventually make us an alcoholic.
Alcoholism has nothing to do with the level of education or socializing, as is often assumed. This disease affects people of all social preconditions. There is the craftsman who treats himself to ten beers every evening after work, the doctor who regularly drinks a bottle of vodka after a hard day's work, the secretary, who relaxes with three or four glasses of wine before bed time due to the high volume of work, or the lawyer whose wife has died, and who can only endure this suffering with alcohol.

Dependency is determined by various factors and causes. This does not happen overnight, but "sneaking up"! No one notices when the limit from socializing drinker to alcoholic has been crossed. Once they have been exceeded, it is too late for a reversal. From this point on, you are the puppet of alcohol and that until you manage to change the "switch" for good. Putting this "switch" will require an enormous effort, effort, and effort to move it into the right area! Very often we are simply overwhelmed with this effort, because we cannot recognize the desired goal due to a lack of information about a life in abstinence! We can no longer begin to imagine what life can be like with a satisfied abstinence. In us, at the time of constant drinking, there is the belief that we could lose alcohol through our "friend" if we renounce it. Through this illusion, it is incredibly difficult for many of us to strip away the shackles of addiction.

This is why it sometimes takes years or even decades for us to be "dry" over a longer period of time.

You don't notice the transition. Nobody notices it, because if you knew exactly, you would go a step further, and you are an alcoholic and you have a terrible, disastrous life ahead of you – no one would then voluntarily become an alcoholic.

Everyone thinks, it does not affect me, it concerns the others, those who have no will. It is often overlooked that the will can only contribute to a longer abstinence to a limited extent. Alcoholism is one of the most enigmatic diseases we know. Few people can cure diseases by their will alone. This also applies to alcoholism.

There can be pressure of addiction, strokes of fate, grief or suffering at lightning speed and without warning. Against such unpredictable disasters, the strongest will often has no chance!

Many of us are so enmeshed in condemning it quickly. "No one has to drink if they don't want to, everyone can get help, others also manage, even guilt, this drunkard, should rip himself together", to name just a few things. But it's not that simple. In my view, this problem is treated too superficially by society and is often lumpen down. It is the circumstances in which we find our way in the course of our lives, which can sometimes be beautiful, but often also very bad and formative. Strokes of fate, depression (also often misunderstood illness), childhood dreams, complexes, domestic violence, mental cruelty, recklessness, bullying, stress, fear, loneliness, burnout, even long-term and many other circumstances can make a person addicted.

But why does it affect some people and some people don't? It can affect people, whose parents have an addiction problem are more prone to addiction than people whose parents do not have this problem. Our genetics also play a major role.

There is a reward system in the brain. Now, when we take a certain substance, this system is designed to have beautiful, pleasant feelings that we want to have again and again. Severe abuse of this substance can result in dependence. This also applies to chocolate, which is far safer than alcohol. In addition, of course, alcohol is part of the fact that alcohol is part of every corner in our society, and is even promoted. I am thinking of the favorable selling prices, I am thinking of folk festivals, parties, discotheques, I am thinking of advertising, I am thinking of the usual trivialization of alcohol. It is not uncommon to see the one who does not want to drink. Other countries sometimes practice a better handling of the poison than Germany. With the nicotine we are already a little further.

The trivialization of alcohol can manipulate our brains and suggest to us that without alcohol one is not one of them. Hardly anyone can imagine a celebration, a reception or even conviviality without alcohol.

Alcohol is not cool and funny! Alcohol is a deadly nerve agent!

German researchers have found that alcohol is significantly more harmful and more deadly than cocaine or heroin, but is still recognized and accepted in society.

Around 21,000 people die each year as a result of alcohol abuse in Germany! In view of these figures, it is incomprehensible that in our country the number one popular drug is still being treated so carefree!

There is no objection to alcohol as a stimulant, but the border is blurred there too, and the abuse is sometimes hard to spot. After all, it cannot be denied that with a certain amount of alcohol something is better to bear. Sometimes you want to go down this supposedly more pleasant way to make grief and suffering more bearable. Or one notices that with alcohol it is easier to talk, inhibitions, fears and the like have disappeared due to this "magic agent"; then you reach for the bottle very quickly without thinking about the consequences.

Our brain is designed to store rewards instantly. It learns to combine drinking with a pleasant feeling. This can be very useful at first, e.g. in stressful situations, depression, inhibition reduction and so on. Alcohol causes a dopamine release that has a targeted effect on the pleasure center. With acute alcohol abuse, more and more nerve cells develop that respond to the drug. The more nerves that are created, the better and faster the alcohol can dock.

Sooner or later, the so-called addiction memory develops. It is not innate and not an independent organ! But this memory remembers exactly how well alcohol has helped in certain situations. Therefore, only a small, seemingly harmless impulse is necessary to bring the memory of addiction to a wake-up even after a very long abstinence and against the will of the person concerned! Every addict has an addiction memory. Now one could simply propose, in a targeted and operational way, perhaps also by means of medication, to eliminate the memory of addiction, and there would be no more alcoholics, and the urge to continue drinking would simply have disappeared. There would be no more processes in the brain that tell the body to give me alcohol, because without it I can't function.

What a beautiful idea. Just live normally. If a party is called for, then drink a little more or less, and the next day is over again. Would it be fantastic if it were medically possible to simply erase the memory of addiction?

But this ominous addiction memory is strongly linked to our emotions! For example, it quickly remembers that with alcohol certain problems such as grief, fear or anger are easier to bear. It also knows exactly how euphoria, joy and even pleasure are increased with the help of the spoon. Medically, as far as I am informed, it is theoretically feasible to erase the memory of addiction. At least it was reportedly successfully tested in rats and mice.

If the "medicine men" were now able to erase the memory of addiction, our emotions might also disappear! Well, I can do without anger, fear or anger. But what about lust for life, passion, joy, wonder or love? Assuming I didn't have those feelings anymore, I wouldn't live properly anymore and wouldn't be human anymore. I am thinking of the "cold heart".

A frightening idea. Then rather be "dry" and stay that keep memory of addiction, but can also live out all the feelings that distinguish us as human beings.

The fatal thing about addiction memory is that it sleeps while we are abstinent. We think it will never wake up again. We think nothing and no one can wake it up. Because if we walk past the liquor rack in the discount store or are at a party where we get a lot of food, when we smell a flag, when we are shown the vodka advertising on TV, then it sleeps. When people pass by completely drunk and have their own memories, when we talk normally about drinking, constantly make jokes about what we were for great "heroes", it sleeps.

But... we do not know when, we cannot foresee it, there are no signs, but at some point, completely out of nowhere, it can awaken, sometimes very slowly, sometimes very quickly, and that is exactly what we must be prepared and prepared for!

If we have now adopted this knowledge, that we have this memory, which always only remembers the great things that we experienced with the "poison" and hardly or not at all about the bad events, then we already have a big advantage. When we know that it can awaken at any time, become hungry and greedy for alcohol, this knowledge is a very good prerequisite for not surrendering to it, but trying to be vigilant at all times, and then to put it back to sleep as soon as possible.

Alcoholics are not people who enjoy hurting their families or other people! With addiction and the resulting drinking, we suddenly change our personality and are no longer the people who were loved by our families when we were not yet dependent. We become unstable, weak, selfish, self-destructive, many of us violent. With what we do, we hurt everyone around us and destroy our environment. The consequence of this is that we are despised, excluded, ignored and isolated. Yes, we are even hated! None of this keeps us from reaching for the bottle again and again!

On normal days I needed three bottles of vodka, sometimes I had to drink a fourth to soothe my body. For some people it can take years to become dependent, others are addicted within half a year! I had my first encounter with my "friend" when I was 15, the first withdrawal symptoms at 18, and when I was 21 years old, the first detox occurred!

It does not necessarily matter the quantity, but primarily the regularity! I met people who "only" drank beer or wine, but basically every day. As a result, these people were given Korsakov syndrome and some of them were no longer able to live their lives independently without outside help.

We need an overall critical approach to alcohol in our society. It is not a weakness to seek help from addictions of any kind! On the contrary, it is a testament to the strength to take this step! Above all, however, we need prevention, which must already be carried out in schools!

In the short term, you can perhaps "fall" by the alcohol or surrender to the intoxication, in the long run it is a killer! Worst of all, there is no repentance! If you find that you can no longer "without", you are addicted and that is forever!

So it is better and absolutely advisable not to enter into a love affair with this deadly friend!

After a felt eternity, I was able to renounce my deadly friend. It was very hard. He still wants to maintain the relationship with me after all that has happened.

It is inevitable for me to avoid him. While shopping, he smiles kindly at me from the shelf. On television, he is greeting me and suggests to me that once I am allowed to do so, he is available at every celebration. I often feel his smell when I meet other people.

I would put myself under a lot of pressure if I tried to evade it. When I see, feel or smell my "friend," I think of how horrible, abhorrent, deplorable and agonizing my relationship with him was. I don't think about the supposedly beautiful things I've experienced with him and try to arrange myself in a world where alcohol is common and present everywhere.

"On smooth waves"

I sit alone in my room and tremble from head to toe, drinking again today, and then it's really over. Everyone got rid of them, I stared at the phone and would be so happy – but no one calls me. In front of me stands the bottle, the beautiful-lethal spoon, I know I have to drink now, but immediately I get bad, so slowly comes the heat, and the effect that sets in, I can now think again. Why does this have to be the case?

Why can't I leave it, they will hate me again, but I drink and drink and drink and know my ship sinks, no matter if they hate me, I don't want to leave it now, I need another drink and know my ship sinks.

The effect subsides so slowly, I tip something in again, the voice in me whispers, hey man, let it be! I don't want to be a loser, think of the beautiful time when I was still with my senses, I'm sorry for myself. I don't see a way out anymore, I can't get out of there anymore, what's going on, I can't do it anymore, I drink the bottle. And pray for his own death, he is so close to me, I already see the white light, I want through this door.

Why can't I leave it, they will hate me again, but I drink and drink and drink and know my ship sinks, no matter if they hate me, I don't want to leave it now, I need another drink and know my ship sinks it.

I wake up in the hospital, already fully fixed again, have no memory, what just happened? The nurse thinks I was lucky, my heart, it didn't beat anymore, they brought me back, thank you, O Lord. My life has been given to me anew, I will not let go of it, I will get down on my knees in my mind and fall into your lap, I know I will not do it alone, grab your hand, O Jesus, would I have recognized you earlier!

I could finally leave it, and no one will hate me, but when I drink again, I know my ship sinks it!

It's so important that I think about it, keep directing my thoughts to what happens when you risk it – and not think about the consequences when I forget what was once and the drought sinks in?

What if I lose myself again, where do I go? I know full well that this would be my end, my fight, it would make no sense!

I hold the new life firmly, as firm as I can, maybe at some point I think back as it started ... The hard times that used to be are past, My ship, it floats on smooth waves, now I'm ready!

Thank you very much!

Many thanks to my translator!

A big thank you to Tinchen, Andrea, Katharina, Jule, Netti, Sandra, Malte, Imke, Sievi and everyone else, who supported me with this book project!

I would like to express my special thanks to my family! My mother, who has suffered so much through me, but has nevertheless given me a very good "basic formatting" and today is an excellent mission statement for me! Thanks to my sister Andrea, my brothers Sebastian and Philipp (Zilli, Billi and Willi), who are happy to be there for me again and give me all help. I love you! The same goes for all relatives and acquaintances who are "walking around" in my family!

A huge thank you to my former wife Martina, who has given me a new chance over the years through her love and endless patience! I would also like to thank my two (step-) sons, who had to endure not a little with me!

I would like to thank from the heart all the paramedics who have very often saved my life through their efforts, to all the policemen who had to accompany me on my way, sometimes not in such a good mood. I thank all the people who have accompanied, encouraged and helped me on my chaotic journey. I would particularly like to highlight my addiction counsellor in Bergen, the social pedagogue and the sports therapist in Serrahn!

A big thank you I would like to address to the KMG Klinikum Güstrow! In particular, I would like to thank station F5! I am thinking of the excellent social therapist, of the excellent ward doctor, of all the nurses and nurses, of the occupational therapist, and also of the cleaners. You have all rebuilt me every time, encouraged me and shown new ways. Thank you!

A heartfelt thanks to the therapists as well as to the remarkable head of the long-term institution "Haus Confidence". Your therapeutic and human help has always given me the courage to look forward and to walk forward.

I say thank you to all my dear Christian brothers and sisters who give me every day new strength to continue this life that I am now allowed to lead!

I thank my AA friends who are always there for me! I would like to thank the addiction counselling in Ribnitz-Damgarten as well as my psychologist!

In the end, I thank my dog "Pauli", who repeatedly asks me to go with him into nature, and I got valuable inspiration for this book ;).

Anyone who wants to contact me in order to participate in prevention, for example, is welcome to do so. We need education in our country on how to deal with alcohol, especially in schools!

If you like contacting me on Facebook, Instagram, Youtube and Co. Or visit my website, I will not prevent it :)

Thank you very much for taking your time for this book!

My second book, "Addiction Is Stronger Than Love," is out in August 2019. This is mainly about addiction and its families.

Blurb:

Co-dependency, a nightmare for parents and siblings, spouses and children! Who doesn't know him? Almost every family has an alcoholic person! As a result, almost everyone is affected by co-dependency. Most of the time, those affected are unaware. Steffen Krumm describes his view of the things he experienced both as an addict and as a co-addict. While writing his debut book, "My Deadly Friend," the author was constantly confronted with co-dependence. Reactions to this first book also revealed that co-dependency was a central theme. Women in particular have revealed their experiences with alcohol-dependent partners. This encouraged him to write a book about this relationship disorder as well. All these experiences are processed in the story of Laura and Holger, who lead an initially happy life with their two children. On the 10th wedding anniversary, she realizes, at first very vaguely, that her marriage is no longer as it used to be. At the latest, when she falls into depression herself and wants to put an end to her life, she begins to make changes. This book describes the perspective of a co-addict, an addict, but also the perspective of parents and children to create an overall impression.

About the author: Steffen Krumm was born in 1967 on the island of Rügen. He discovered his love of writing in 2018 and revealed his disastrous life in his debut book, "My Deadly Friend." He wants to draw attention to the enormous power of alcohol and is committed to education and prevention.

Phone: 0176 46604243

steffenk67@gmail.com

Website: https://www.sk-newdreams.de

Printed in Great Britain
by Amazon